GREAT WAR BRITAIN
NORTHAMPTON
Remembering 1914–18

NORTHAMPTON

Remembering 1914–18

PHILIP SAWFORD

The
History
Press

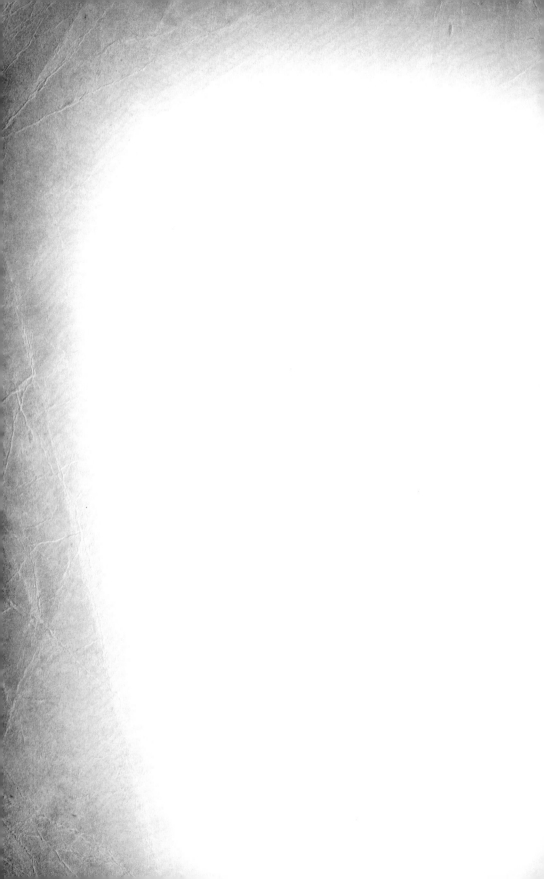

In a Corner of a Foreign Field

Plain wooden crosses, on that field of dead,
Past which the struggling armies long since fled;

Dies down the sound of battle, out of sight,
Save when the bursting flame lights up the night.

Summer and winter pass, and gay birds sing,
Touching this place of death with joy of spring …

Written by the sister of a Northampton officer.
Published in the Northampton Independent *in 1919.*

This book is dedicated to the memory of the men,
women and children of Northampton who endured
the human catastrophe that was the First World War.

First published 2015

The History Press
The Mill, Brimscombe Port
Stroud, Gloucestershire, GL5 2QG
www.thehistorypress.co.uk

British Library Cataloguing in Publication Data.
A catalogue record for this book is available from the British Library.

ISBN 978 0 7509 6154 7

Typesetting and origination by The History Press
Printed and bound in Malta, by Melita Press.

CONTENTS

TIMELINE

1914

28 June

Assassination of Archduke
Franz Ferdinand in Sarajevo

4 August

Great Britain declares war on Germany

8 August

200 horses from Northampton are requisitioned
by the army and sent via train to the
Northamptonshire Regiment's camp at Shorncliffe

11 August

Beds at Northampton Hospital
are offered to wounded soldiers

13 August

The 1st Battalion sail from England for France
as part of the British Expeditionary Force

23 August

Battle of Tannenberg commences

6 September

First Battle of the Marne

19 October

First Battle of Ypres

1915

25 April

Allied landing at Gallipoli

7 May

Germans torpedo and
sink the Lusitania

9 May

The Battle of Aubers Ridge.
The Northamptonshire
Regiment takes heavy losses

31 May

First German Zeppelin
raid on London

11 October

Responsibility for Pattishall
internment camp is handed over
to the military authorities

20 December

Allies finish their evacuation of
and withdrawal from Gallipoli

1916

24 January

*The British Government
introduces conscription*

21 February

Battle of Verdun commences

31 May

Battle of Jutland

4 June

Brusilov Offensive commences

1 July

*First day of the Battle of the Somme
with 57,000 British casualties*

27 August

Italy declares war on Germany

18 December

Battle of Verdun ends

1917

6 April

The United States declares war on Germany

9 April

Battle of Arras

4 July

*1st Battalion Northamptonshire
Regiment take heavy losses during
the Battle of the Dunes*

31 July

Third Battle of Ypres (Passchendaele)

*Lieutenant Colonel Mobbs is killed
whilst leading his men from the front*

20 August

Third Battle of Verdun

19 October

*A Zeppelin raid on Northampton kills
three members of the Gammons family*

26 October

Second Battle of Passchendaele

20 November

Battle of Cambrai

7 December

*USA declares war on
Austria-Hungary*

1918

3 March

Russia and the Central Powers sign the Treaty of Brest-Litovsk

21 March

Second Battle of the Somme

15 July

Second Battle of the Marne

8 August

Battle of Amiens, first stage of the Hundred Days Offensive

22 September

The Great Allied Balkan victory

27 September

Storming of the Hindenburg Line

8 November

Armistice negotiations commence

9 November

Kaiser Wilhelm II abdicates, Germany is declared a Republic

11 November

Armistice Day, cessation of hostilities on the Western Front

News of the Armistice reaches Northampton. Ecstatic crowds gather in the Market Square to sing patriotic songs

1919

22 March

Last wounded man leaves Duston War Hospital

6 September

Heroes Day parade through the town centre. A celebratory feast is held in Abington Park

1999

11 July

A memorial to ex-Cobbler's player Walter Tull is unveiled at Sixfields

ACKNOWLEDGEMENTS

My thanks are due to the following people:

Jane Seddon and Vicki Davies at Northampton Museums & Art Gallery. Sandra Bemrose for her information about Duston War Hospital and permission to publish diaries. Ben Brown at Sywell Aviation Museum. Sue Longworth, Jenny Butterfield, Chris Kimbell and Julia Corps at Northampton Hospital Archive. Deborah Mason at the Rugby Football Union for her help and permission to publish photographs from their collection. Peter Mounfield for allowing his statistics on shoe production to be published via Northampton Shoe Museum. The staff at No. 78 Derngate for their information on Bassett Lowke. The staff at the County Records Office, the staff at the Central Library Northampton and the staff at the National Archives.

INTRODUCTION

I must admit that before I started to research this book I had a very limited knowledge of life on the home front during the Great War. Like most people, I knew about the trenches, the great battles at sea and about the air aces but I knew very little about life for those who were left behind.

Wartime recruitment poster. (Library of Congress, LC-USZC4-10881)

What I have come to realise about the First World War is that it was truly a people's war. This is something that I knew about the Second World War but not about the Great War. I knew about air raids, rationing and civil defence in the Second World War but I didn't know that all of these things had happened during the Great War. The more I researched the more I realised that the public's contribution to war was just as vital as those fighting abroad.

The people of Northampton contributed to victory in a range of different ways. War committees were formed. Money was raised for a range of causes: prisoners of war, cigarettes for

These regimental symbols have been hand carved out of soft chalk by men at the front.

the troops, memorials to honour the war dead and many more besides. Women volunteered for positions such as VAD nurses whilst men volunteered as Special Constables. Ordinary people gave up space in their homes for Belgian refugees. The population had to endure unprecedented inflation, rationing and even attack from Zeppelins.

Compared with the great suffering experienced by the men of the town who went away to fight, the plight of the citizens of Northampton pales into insignificance, but that does not mean that it should be forgotten. Many books have been written about the men who went off to fight but few have been written about those who stayed behind. This book seeks to try and redress the issue by looking at some of the ways that the Great War affected the people of Northampton. It is by no means exhaustive. I have tried, as far as possible, to reflect a different range of issues in bite-sized sections.

The images in this book are from a range of sources but are mainly drawn from the collection of Northampton Museums & Art Gallery, the Northamptonshire Regiments Museum and the collection of the Northamptonshire Yeomanry.

Philip Sawford, 2015

1

OUTBREAK OF WAR

You will all damned well wish it was over long before it is!

*Captain E.J. Needham, 3rd Battalion Northamptonshire Regiment,
attached to the 1st Battalion, remembering the comments of
fellow officer Guy Robinson on the announcement of war*

August Bank Holiday Weekend

The commencement of war did not come as a shock on 4 August 1914. For many months previously the tension in Europe had been escalating. The topic on the nation's lips was not whether there would be a war in Europe but whether Great Britain could avoid involvement. As the situation in Europe was coming to a head over the August bank holiday weekend, the people of Northampton enjoyed the summer weather and a host of local entertainment whilst blissfully unaware of how their everyday lives would soon be changed forever. On 1 August 1914 the *Northampton Independent* reported:

Amid this aggregation of woe it is difficult to work up the proper holiday spirit, but there are no signs in Northampton at all events that people will stay at home in consequence. The luggage-loaded precessions to the stations have started and I am assured on authority that the bookings are already above the average.

The same article also tells us that the prospect of a holiday was becoming more achievable for those who worked in the shoe industry due to the recent rises in wages and the newfound cheapness of travel. Other events reported in the *Independent* prior to the outbreak of war include Northampton's 24th cycle parade. The event, which raised money for the hospital, consisted of a themed bicycle-mounted costumed competition. The winner for 1914 was Miss Lucy Talby of Burton Latimer who was dressed, rather aptly, as 'Purity'. Other news included the results of the ladies swimming championship, which was held in the Nene by Northampton Life Saving Society, and there was also a local baby show.

These were among some of the last articles that detailed the social activities of a peaceful town, before the commencement of the largest and most deadly war in the history of the British people. It would be another four and a quarter years before the local newspapers were once again filled with such ordinary, mundane but peaceful news.

On Sunday, 2 August 1914, news from London was slowly trickling into Northampton. Many people were gathering in the town centre in a bid to try and gather any news that they could. The reports from London were becoming increasingly more serious. The people of Northampton started to realise that it was unlikely that Great Britain would not be involved in the coming conflict. The war clouds had started to block out the peaceful bank holiday sun.

On Monday, 3 August 1914, the *Northampton Daily Echo* reported:

Though the whole town was intensely excited by the war news given in the Sunday morning papers and by the important telegraphs pasted outside the *Daily Echo* office at intervals during the day, there was a gratifying absence of the wild scenes which marked the preliminary stages of the South African campaign. There was abundant evidence that practically everyone realised the extreme gravity of the struggle just commencing, and while not shaking the issue everyone hoped that England might be able to keep a free hand.

Abington Square before the outbreak of war. Note the absence of the town war memorial that was constructed in the early 1920s.

In the New Theatre, where a concert was being given by the band of the Grenadier Guards, the news brought about a more jingoistic response. As the band played 'Rule Britannia', many within the concert stood to attention and joined in with the rousing lyrics.

War is Declared

On Tuesday, 4 August 1914, official notice was given that war had been declared. Britain, along with her allies, was at war with Germany and the Central Powers. In an age without mobile telephones and mass media, the news trickled around the streets of Northampton with ever-growing pace and excitement. At the County Ground, Northamptonshire were playing Leicestershire in a cricket match at the time that war broke out. One of the Leicestershire players, by the name of Aubrey Sharp, left straight away, despite being halfway through the match, in order to join his regiment. It was reported that his actions brought many disparaging comments from the spectators, who believed that it was not such a great emergency that he could not have finished the match first.

Frederick William Henry Holmes, even years after the war, could clearly remember the day that war was announced. He was making the most of the bank holiday weekend by boating on the Nene with his young friends when someone shouted from the embankment that war had been declared. He recalled nothing but excitement about the whole affair. In these early days the people of Britain were in no way prepared for the terrible reality of the Great War and the newspapers were speculating that the conflict would only last for six months.

Not everyone was lucky enough to be safely at home when war was declared. Mr E. Wright, who was representing Messrs Phipps and Sons at Frankfurt, just managed to catch the last train for Belgium. He was on the same train as German soldiers who had been mobilised. They commandeered the refreshments carriage and Mr Wright was half starved by the time he made it to the Belgian border.

Mr Harold Wilkinson, who was an officer in the Ambulance Brigade, was on holiday with his wife in Belgium when the war started. They were totally unaware of the outbreak of war and when they asked for directions in Namur, Belgium, they aroused suspicion and were arrested as spies. Luckily their identities and honest intentions were confirmed and they were eventually released and put straight on a train for their own protection.

The Territorial soldiers of the 4th Northamptonshire Regiment were at Ashbridge Park in Hertfordshire with the East Midland Territorial Brigade when war was declared. They received orders to break camp and to return to Northampton immediately. When they reached Northampton train station at three o'clock in the afternoon they were greeted by a large cheering crowd. The same scene greeted them in every street as they marched to the Territorial Headquarters in Clare Street. All Territorial and Reservist soldiers received orders to report to their barracks. Many soldiers had already packed their bags and equipment in anticipation and were ready to go as soon as they received their orders. To cope with the increased number of troop movements, the London and North Western Railways cancelled all pre-booked excursions, leaving many unhappy customers in Northampton.

By Wednesday, 5 August 1914, the town's barracks started to fill with troops. Approximately 350 troops of the 930-strong 4th

Battalion Northamptonshire Regiment had reached the Territorial Headquarters. The Wellingborough and Kettering detachments of the regiment reached the town over the next couple of days. The *Northampton Daily Echo* printed an interview with a Territorial Army officer who confidently stated that, 'the men are now up and will probably be in uniform for six months'.

Public Reaction, Panic Buying and Shortages

On 15 August 1914 the first adverts for 'war goods' appeared in the *Northampton Independent*. Brice and Sons Ltd, of the Drapery, were advertising 'comforts for the brave', which included flannels, sheeting, towels and various other essentials for those joining the forces.

Newspaper snippets from the *Northamptonshire Independent*, 1 August 1914:

Abington Park Concert season 1914. Sunday August 2nd. Band of the Grenadier Guards. Enclosure 6*d* and 3*d*. In case of wet concert held in the New Theatre.

Northampton Turkish Baths. Tickets: 2/6 till 5pm; 1/6 after 5pm. An ideal health-giving luxury.

Madam Wright, court hairdresser from Regent Street London, just opened a ladies hairdressing salon at 2 Abington Street.

On 23 August an open-air and multi-denominational church service was held in Abington Park to pray for 'the welfare of the Allies and an entreaty for divine guidance for the British nation'. The service was said to have attracted the largest congregation ever seen at a public worship in the town. A collection was held and it raised the sum of £77 for the Red Cross. This was probably the first instance of money being raised for the war effort in the town. It was the start of a tradition of fund-raising that would continue for the rest of the war. A Red Cross Week was held each year for the duration of the war.

Upon hearing the declaration of war, the people of Northampton (like many others around the country) continued a long-held tradition in times of national emergency and went straight out to buy as many goods as they possibly could to stock up their supplies. Grocers soon had queues forming outside their shops as they struggled to keep up with demand. It was reported by one local grocer that an order had been placed for £100-worth of foodstuffs by a local estate and that private cars were sent to collect the orders.

On the Saturday following the declaration of war, for the first time in living memory, there was no corn on offer at the Corn Market. Cattle at the market were fetching an extra £2–3 a head more than the previous week, and similarly wheat that had been going for 25*s* the previous week was selling for 35*s*. As a result, bread went from 2½*d* to 3*d* a loaf. Sugar went from 2*d* to 4*d* per lb. The panic buying did soon die down, however, and goods, for a time, returned to their pre-war prices.

In October 1914, the British Red Cross and the St John Ambulance Brigade formed the Joint War Committee. The committee decided that the two organisations would merge to combine their efforts for the duration of the war for the greater good of the town and the nation.

Joining Up

On 7 August, Lord Kitchener appealed for 100,000 men aged between 19 and 30 to join the army. Old soldiers, especially non-commissioned officers (NCOs), up to the age of 42 years were also asked to join. Within two weeks the target of 100,000 men had been more than exceeded. The mood of many of these early recruits could probably be summed up by the words of Charles Crutchley, who 'wanted to be in the fight of right against might, [and to] teach the Germans a lesson, and get the business over as quickly as possible'. In order to meet the rush of volunteers coming forward, a recruiting office was opened at the Northamptonshire Depot Barracks on Barrack Road.

Charles Keightley, who later went on to serve in B Company 6th Battalion Northants, was among those who answered Kitchener's call. Along with four friends from G.T. Hawkin's boot factory, he made his way to the recruiting office. They were met with a very long queue of men who had all come forward to volunteer. After filling in the required paperwork and going for a medical, they were sent before Major Hughes in order to take the Oath of Allegiance. The system set up to process recruits was unable to cope with the large numbers who had volunteered, however, and the situation was not helped by the medical officer passing people as fit quicker than the major could swear them in. The major could only process one man at a time as they only had one Bible. In order to

RATES OF PAY FOR A PRIVATE SOLDIER
A new private soldier joining an infantry regiment could only expect to earn 1s per day. From this pay he would have to account for any further deductions, such as barrack damage. If he was caught in a state of drunkenness, according to the King's Regulations, he could be fined 2s 6d for a first offence and 5s for the second!

speed up the attestation process, the major decided to swear four men in at once, each man holding on to one corner of the Bible. Luckily for Keightley, one of his comrades did not pass the medical, leaving only four of the original group and meaning that they could start their army careers together rather than one man being sworn in alone.

Once the new recruits had been sworn in they were paraded on the square and issued with instructions to go home, pack and to report back on Saturday afternoon. On Saturday the new recruits were marched through the town to the railway station. They boarded a train to London and made their way to Shorncliffe Camp in Kent. There they were housed with eight men to a tent. Some recruits had to wait for weeks to get any equipment at all and even the basics, such as eating utensils, plates and bowls, were not always available. A couple of veterans actually recalled getting tins out of the rubbish bins in order to use them as makeshift cups. Eventually they were given some money to go into town to buy civilian overcoats and then they were issued with an intermediate 'Kitchener Blue' uniform. These uniforms were made to the same cut as the regular army uniforms but, as there was a shortage in khaki-coloured material, blue was used as an alternative. Weapons

'For King and Country.' Picture postcards like this one of the Kettering Road were sold to troops billetted in the town.

were also in short supply at this stage and basic arms drill was carried out using wooden dummy weapons. The young conscripts wearing blue Kitchener Blue uniforms, civilian coats and carrying wooden training rifles must have been a rather sorry sight to behold.

The army was not just short of uniforms and equipment but also of trained leaders. As a result, anyone with experience of leading men or with a basic knowledge of military skills was often fast-tracked to become an officer. Captain E.F. Stokes was one of those officers: 'I was a school master with no military experience save the membership of the Cambridge University Officer Training Corps but found myself, on Colonel Ripley's nomination, a second Lieutenant.' The Officer Training Corps were based at universities and public schools and predated the war. The corps was designed to give young men an insight into military skills and to instil discipline in preparation for a future career in the army. The officers needed support in the form of NCOs. These men would help the officer in the day-to-day management of the other ranks. Men who had been a shop foreman, a Boy Scout or anyone who had any other form of leadership credential found themselves being promoted to the rank of a NCO.

Guy Paget, an ex-regular officer of the Scots Guards, arrived at Shoreham Camp to find the men that Edgar Mobbs – a well-known local rugby football player – had helped to raise. He had 1,000 men and some tents but nothing that looked like a military unit. He later recalled:

Local photography studios did a good trade taking photographs of newly kitted out volunteers before they went off to fight.

> I divided them up into four lots according to where they came from. I asked for old NCOs and about five stepped forward. Then about a score of old soldiers broke rank and they were all made sergeants on the spot. When I got to the footballers, not a man moved. I made Edgar Mobbs Company Sergeant Major, his four best friends Platoon Sergeants and all the Boy Scouts were made Corporals. The five old NCOs became RQMSs [Regimental Quartermaster Sergeants] and CSMs [Company Sergeant Majors].

Edgar Mobbs

Edgar Mobbs was a well-known and well-respected rugby football player before the First World War. He had a long and interesting career playing for a number of different rugby teams as well as playing cricket and hockey. He captained the East Midlands, Northampton and the England Rugby Union teams. In 1913, at the age of 31, he retired from the sport and followed his father into the auto trade, becoming the manager of the Pytchley Auto Car Company. On the outbreak of war, Mobbs tried to enlist in the army as an officer, however, due to his age, he was turned down for a commission. Not to be deterred, he enlisted as a private and set about helping to raise men for the new 7th (Service) Battalion. Due to his fame on the rugby field, Mobbs was able to encourage 400 men from the town to enlist with him in a period of only forty-eight hours! Of the 400 men that came forward, 250 of them were selected as being suitable. These new recruits formed D Company of the 7th Battalion and soon became known as Mobbs' Own.

By April 1916 Mobbs had worked his way up the ranks to command the battalion as a lieutenant colonel. His swift rise up the rank structure was not just a product of the army's rapidly increasing size and heavy losses, but also because of his charismatic leadership skills. Earl Spencer summed up Mobbs' attributes succinctly when he said, 'he was a most admirable organiser, a patriotic man (and) a born solider'. Mobbs was killed on 31 July 1917, whilst displaying the very attributes that ensured his rapid promotion. His battalion had become bogged down whilst attacking a German position and, without fear for his own safety, Mobbs set off with his runner in order to ascertain the exact position of the German machine gun that was proving to be so trouble-some for his men. Upon moving forward, Mobbs was mortally wounded in the neck by a bullet. As he lay injured he continued his task and proceeded to write out the exact locations of the machine gun. This lack of concern for his own safety and the desire to do the best for his men was a constant theme during his time as an officer. The news of his death was not just a blow for the men of his battalion but, as Lord Lilford suggested, 'The death of Colonel Mobbs would bring sorrow into every home in Northampton.' Mobbs' body was never recovered and as a result he has no known grave.

Team picture from an England v. Wales rugby game in 1909.
Edgar Mobbs is pictured sitting in the second row, second in from the right.

Malcolm Ernest Hancock, of the 4th (Territorial) Battalion the Northamptonshire Regiment, joined up on 13 April 1915. After serving in the Officer Training Corps at Wellingborough School, he joined the army as an officer. Hancock later recalled the hurriedness of his training. He was posted directly to his unit, which at the time were based in Norwich, and was told that he had to lead his men, who he was yet to meet, in a march-past. Up to that point the only training that he had received was in the Officer Training Corps and he'd never marched past anything before, let alone a commanding officer.

Unlike enlisted men, officers were expected to not only acquire their own uniform but to pay for it as well. An allowance was made to cover the cost of such items but, in reality, it was often not enough to cover the full amount. A young officer could purchase his uniform from a variety of tailors within the town. Many of these tailors advertised their services in the local

An identification disc, often known as a dog tag, as issued to a private in the Northamptonshire Regiment. Once joined up, men were given a unique army number for identification purposes. This number – along with their name, regiment and religion – were stamped on to the metal disc and the disc was then worn around the neck.

papers. Alongside a photograph of a dashing young officer, A.E. Towers, of No. 32 the Drapery and No. 12 Market Square, promoted themselves as a 'military tailor and outfitter'. A service dress jacket would cost £3 30s, a pair of slacks £1 10s and a service cap could be purchased at 10s 6d. For those wishing to upgrade their kit, a raincoat could also be purchased at £3 15s. Many of the tailors also stocked essentials such as a camp cot, portable washbasin and various other luxurious items. For families whose relations were already at the front, the items could be sent directly to the front line as long as a regimental address was provided. Many letters home to loved ones included small shopping lists of items to be purchased from such establishments.

Although the initial recruitment of officers was along the traditional class lines, as the war progressed and the number of casualties increased, men from the ranks, with the required leadership skills, were given field promotions. One famous and remarkable example of this is Walter Tull. Tull was originally from London and was a professional football player who used to play for Tottenham Hotspur before transferring to play for Northampton Town Football Club. In 1914, when war was declared, Tull enlisted as a private in the now famous Footballer's Battalion of the Middlesex Regiment. He rose through the ranks rapidly and his leadership skills led him to be recommended for a commission as an officer. The achievement of crossing the class divide between working-class private soldier and gentleman officer was even more remarkable in Edwardian Britain due to the fact that Walter Tull was of Afro-Caribbean origin. On 30 May 1917, Tull became the first British-born black officer in the British Army. Unfortunately, Tull never did return to play for Northampton as he was killed on 25 March 1918 on the Somme whilst helping his men to retreat to safety.

Of all of the major belligerents in the war, Britain was the only one to rely upon volunteers as the means of supplying recruits for the Armed Forces. However, the early rush of men to the recruiting stations in the first months of the war could not be maintained. In 1915, as casualty figures mounted, recruiting was still on a large scale but not nearly as great as in 1914. Towards the end of 1915, the authorities, fearing inadequate military personnel, started to move towards the European model of mass conscription. Reluctant to bring in such a system, a compromise was reached in the form of the Derby Scheme of October 1915.

The Derby Scheme and the Military Service Act

A red crown armband as issued to the men who signed up to the Derby Scheme. The armband was intended to show that the man wearing it had attested and was prepared to fight in the future as and when they were needed. Like the Silver War Badge, it was a way of proving that the wearer was doing 'their bit' for the war effort.

The Derby Scheme, introduced in October 1915, was designed to ascertain whether enough volunteers could be found to make conscription unnecessary. Those men who were prepared to serve in the future were asked to attest their willingness to do so. The advantage of this scheme for the men who came forward to attest was that they were issued with a khaki armband bearing a red crown, which was worn on the left arm as a symbol of their attestment.

In the event, not enough men attested and, as a result, conscription was introduced by the Military Service Act in January 1916. Initially it covered single men aged between 18 and 41. The act was later amended in May 1916 to include married men. Tribunals, headed by local noteworthy people, were set up as a result of the Military Service Act to hear the appeals of those who felt that

their conscription into the armed forces was unjust due to their religious beliefs or due to personal circumstances. The military tribunals are discussed in a later chapter. Of all of the men that served their country during the Great War the vast majority of them served with the army and nearly half of its recruits came in the period of voluntary enlistment.

Recruiting Posters

When the initial influx of volunteers had started to diminish, the government tried to increase the number of recruits for the army by publishing a range of recruitment posters. Many of these posters were far from subtle. The words 'Go! It's your duty lad', printed next to a picture of a mother and son, hoped to persuade both generations that it was a young man's duty to enlist to fight. Another poster asked wives, 'When the war is over and someone asks your husband or your son what he did in the Great War, is he to hang his head because you would not let him go?' This official government propaganda was backed by the patriotic editorial columns in the local and national newspapers. The columnists praised those who had volunteered to go and fight, and poured scorn on those who the columnists labelled as 'war dodgers'. Some young men had good reasons for not enlisting. In an age before the National Health Service and other social benefits that we enjoy today, some young men had to look after their families either financially or physically and in some cases both. Such young men were wrongfully subjected to these types of accusations for the duration of the war.

The White Feather Brigade and Propaganda

On 30 August 1914, Charles Penrose Fitzgerald, a retired admiral, started the famous white feather campaign. A white feather has traditionally been a sign of cowardice and Fitzgerald deputised thirty women in Folkstone to hand out white feathers to any man who was not in uniform in order to shame 'every young slacker found loafing about ...' The women who presented men with white feathers were soon after referred to as the White Feather Brigade. This local campaign soon spread nationwide; Northampton included.

Edward Henry Tyler Robinson was a junior reporter for the *Northampton Echo* and one of many men who decided to join the army after an encounter with one of the White Feather Brigade. He later recalled that within the space of one week in April 1915 he had been given three white feathers by 'Middle aged [women who were] a bit aggressive'. Upon gaining his third feather, he told his friend that he was going to toss a coin and if it came down heads he would go up to the Racecourse, where the recruitment office was located, and join up. Unfortunately for Edward, the coin came down heads up. Although only 17½, he stuck to his word and duly went to the recruiter. Upon telling the recruiting sergeant his age, he was told, 'walk three times around the Racecourse and you'll be a bit older and you can enlist'. At that time new entrants into the army had to be at least 19 years of age.

A novelty picture postcard with a serious message. The handwritten message on the reverse says: 'I'm showing you the difference between a khaki boy and a civil man. A civil man was sitting in a tank while the khaki boy was fighting for him and his country.'

Hi, there! You ought to be in Khaki!
Well, I'm in a tank, conshtable, so I'm alrigh', aint I?

Frederick William Henry Holmes of Kingsthorpe was also approached by numerous strangers and asked why he wasn't in uniform; again despite the fact that he was too young to join up. When the Derby Scheme was launched, Frederick and two older friends thought that it would be an adventure to sign up to the new scheme and join the forces. By 1915, Frederick was only 18 years old and so he lied about his age in order to enlist. All three of them wanted to join the Northamptonshire Yeomanry for no reason other than that they had a smarter uniform than the infantry.

Silver War Badge

The Silver War Badge was instituted in 1916 as a way of helping men who had seen military service from being called a coward or a war dodger. The badge was awarded to any man who had been honourably discharged from military service and was retrospectively given to those discharged during the period from 1914 to 1915. The badge was only to be worn on civilian clothes and was to be worn on the right lapel. A man could be discharged from military service for a variety of reasons; the most common reason for being discharged was due to being permanently psychically unfit for service. Men who had been injured due to their service but had no outward physical problem could wear the Silver War Badge in public as a way of showing that they had done their duty. Over 1 million of these badges were awarded during the war. The badge bore the royal cipher of King George V surrounded by the words: 'For King and Empire – Services Rendered.' On the reverse, the badges were individually engraved with a unique number.

This Silver War Badge belonged to 38801 Private (Pte) Ralph of the Northamptonshire Regiment. The roll of individuals entitled to the War Badge tells us that Pte Ralph enlisted on 20 February 1917 and was discharged on 31 May 1917 due to 'sickness'.

2

PREPARATIONS AT HOME

DORA

(1) His Majesty in Council has power during the continuance of the present war to issue regulations as to the powers and duties of the Admiralty and Army Council, and of the members of His Majesty's forces, and other persons acting in his behalf, for securing the public safety and the defence of the realm; and may, by such regulations, authorise the trial by courts martial and punishment of persons contravening any of the provisions of such regulations designed:

(a) To prevent persons communicating with the enemy or obtaining information for that purpose or any purpose calculated to jeopardise the success of the operations of any of His Majesty's forces or to assist the enemy; or

(b) To secure the safety of any means of communication, or of railways, docks or harbours; in like manner as if such persons were subject to military law and had on active service committed an offence under section 5 of the Army Act.

The Defence of the Realm Act, 8 August 1914

The Defence of the Realm Act (DORA) also brought about the introduction of British Summer Time, which gave farmers more daylight time in which to harvest their crops. Another requirement was for public houses to water down beer, to shut for a couple of hours each afternoon and to ban the purchasing of rounds, perhaps in an effort to avoid the divulgence of valuable information over one too many pints. It also became illegal to purchase binoculars, melt down gold or silver and to trespass on railway lines or bridges.

COUNTY BOROUGH OF NORTHAMPTON.

NOTICE
TO
KEEPERS OF PIGEONS.

No Person shall, in the United Kingdom, keep or have in his possession any CARRIER OR HOMING PIGEONS, unless he has obtained from the Chief Officer of Police of the District a Permit for the purpose (which Permit may at any time be revoked), and the Chief Officer of Police, may, if he considers it necessary or expedient to do so, cause any pigeons kept in contravention of this Regulation to be liberated.

These steps are taken in pursuance of the King's Proclamation and the Acts passed by Parliament for the defence of the Realm.

Application should at once be made for a Permit by any Person to whom this Order refers, to the Central Police Station, Dychurch Lane.

For non-compliance with this Regulation a person is liable to be arrested without a warrant and tried by Court Martial.

F. H. MARDLIN,
CHIEF CONSTABLE.

Central Police Station,
Northampton,
2nd November, 1914.

The Defence of the Realm Act (DORA) even prevented members of the public from keeping homing pigeons without a license.

DORA was revised six times throughout the duration of the Great War. The amendments to the Act were often due to particular events. The deadliness of Zeppelin raids, for instance, forced the government into action. As of 10 January 1916 the people of Northampton were required, by order of the 'naval and military authorities', to ensure that their household's windows, skylights and doors did not show more than a 'dull subdued light'. It was recommended that dark-coloured curtains or blinds were used to ensure that this new regulation was not breached. Those who could afford a motorcar, and were able to get some petrol for it, were told that the use of headlights was completely forbidden.

These regulations had been brought in to counter the increasing threat from German air raids. Such raids were first carried out by Zeppelins and then later in the war by multi-engine Gotha bombers. The first raid of the war had been on the towns of Great Yarmouth, Sheringham and King's Lynn on the night of 19–20 January 1915. By 1916 the Zeppelins were coming further inland towards the industrial heart of England. This meant that the people of Northamptonshire had to start taking the same precautions that many people who lived on the coast had been used to for some time. The threat of Zeppelins was made apparent in late 1917 when the town was bombed. This tragedy, which cost the lives of three civilians, is discussed in detail later on in the book.

Enemies Within Our Midst

On 22 August, the *Northampton Independent* reported that a young German man, who had been living and working in the town on the Kettering Road, had withdrawn money from a bank and had left town. Upon visiting his house, in order to register him as a German citizen living within the borough, it was discovered that he had erected a radio on the roof without a license. It cannot be determined who the gentleman was, nor can it be determined if his radio had been used for clandestine purposes, but what is clear is that the people of Northampton were becoming increasing paranoid about 'enemies within their midst'.

Hannover-born Julius Gottschalk also caused a stir in the town due to his nationality. For many years he had been in charge of the town's tramways. He had rendered many years of faithful service to the town but at the start of the war, public opinion turned and many people suggested that he should be removed from his post. To many people in the town, the idea of having a German in charge of the tramways was unacceptable. The story even reached the national newspapers, including *The Times*. It was argued that he had kept the trams running very well and that he was very effective in his post, but others pointed out that he knew too much about the bridges and roads and was, therefore, a potential security risk. The *Northampton Independent* even went as far as to list the two sides of the argument for Gottschalk's dismissal. One of the arguments for keeping him in his post was that 'He married an English lady, who is now dead, and one of his sons has served in the British Army', whilst a slightly less considered argument for his dismissal simply stated, 'Once a German always a German!'

The problem for Mr Gottschalk was that although he had lived a large proportion of his life in England he had never officially applied to be a British citizen via naturalisation. Although committed to Britain, he was still officially a German. The council held a meeting to decide Mr Gottschalk's future and a vote concerning his dismissal ended in deadlock, with a casting vote refusing to be placed. In the end, the council allowed him to offer his resignation of his own accord and provided him with £300 compensation. This gesture did not go down well with many people and he endured many insults in the streets. As a result Mr Gottschalk, along with his family, left the town. They did, however, eventually return to Northampton.

Neither of these cases were particularly unusual at the time. Many German people had come to Britain before the war in order to find jobs. The 1911 census for Northampton tells us that there were twenty-eight Germans living in Northampton; one of whom was a British subject, three had become a citizen through naturalisation, whilst twenty-four were categorised as foreigners. In and amongst various other nationalities there were also six Austrians and two Hungarians recorded in the 1911 census.

DORA
On 4 August the *Northampton Daily Chronicle* reported that the Northampton wireless station had been dismantled by the local post office engineers by order of the Post Master General.

PATTISHALL PRISONER-OF-WAR CAMP

What would become known as Pattishall prisoner-of-war camp initially started out as a detention centre. German 'aliens' were rounded up by order of the Chief Constable of Northamptonshire and arrangements were made for Eastcote House near Pattishall to be made available to receive approximately sixty people. Initially, the camp was run by the National Sailors' and Firemen's Union and not by the War Office. The camp originally housed merchant seaman who had been interned following the outbreak of war. By 1915 the union had 289 men at Eastcote. The security in the early days of the camp was limited and a number of internees managed to escape, though only one actually made it to the east coast.

The camp was handed over to the military authorities on 11 October 1915. By the end of 1916 the civilian internees had been transferred to other camps and Eastcote became a prisoner-of-war camp. Over time the camp grew in size and, by 3 May 1919, 4,509 prisoners were recorded as being detained. The camp was very well constructed, with two layers of barbed-wire fencing keeping the prisoners in and with sleeping huts, dining halls and entertainment facilities. The prisoners even constructed a model boating lake with a model watermill and kept a series of allotments. What is also worthy of note is that the camp was supplied with electric lighting via an onsite generator whilst Pattishall village had to wait until the 1930s to get a mains electricity supply. The site had everything that it needed to be self-sufficient. It had its own bakery and kitchens, carpentry shop and even a theatre where the prisoners put on shows and concerts. Other entertainment was supplied in the form of craft activities. The prisoners produced a range of different craft items such as models and toys, which were traded with the local population.

*Interned sailors at East Cote internee camp,
later known as Pattishall prisoner-of-war camp.*

War Horses

Within days of the outbreak of war, horses used for pulling carts and wagons through the streets of Northampton were being commandeered by the army for war service. The army of 1914 relied heavily upon horses, not just for their cavalry regiments but also to draw their supply wagons and artillery pieces. In addition to these heavy-duty horses, the army also needed top-quality horses for its officers and cavalry regiments. Such horses were provided locally by the Pytchley Hunt, which was famous for the quality of its hunting horses, and Lord Rothschild gave all the horses from his local estate. The owners of horses that had been requisitioned were entitled to compensation for their loss. The top recorded price noted in the local newspapers for a horse was £70. Each horse was paid for in accordance with a grading system. The better the quality of the horse, the greater the price the army would pay for it. The prices most commonly paid were £20, £25 and £35. A good polo pony would be purchased at £25. If a horse's owner was unhappy about the price paid then they had the right to appeal.

Hay and fodder for the horses at the Racecourse. All of the army's heavy equipment was horse-drawn for the majority of the war.

No 519 THE HORSES WELSH R.F.A.

On 8 August it was reported that nearly 200 horses had been obtained and then dispatched at the train station bound for the Northamptonshire Regiment's horse depot at Shorncliffe Camp. Before departing they were stored at the Cattle Market. The same article predicted that another 200 horses would be taken in the coming weeks in order to equip the Northamptonshire Yeomanry.

The Racecourse was soon ruined by the number of horses that were kept there all year round.

The Burden of Billeting

On 29 August the local papers announced that 16,000 soldiers of the Welsh Division, along with their 7,000 horses, were beginning to arrive in the town. By September 1914 over 20,000 soldiers had moved to the borough and the surrounding area. In addition to draining the local food supplies, the troops had to be housed in and around the town as the existing barracks were not sufficient to take all of the new troops. In 1914 there were 20,900 houses in the town. Sergeant E.H. Hare of the Cheshire Regiment recalled that he was billeted in the working-class district of Far Cotton, where in some cases men were squeezed three to a bed. He took the decision to sleep outside on some waste ground where he would at least get space if not comfort.

He would then spend his army pay of 1s a day in Northampton on food; otherwise it was army food, cooked and eaten in the open. This boost in trade was reported in the local papers with small traders such as tobacconists, newsagents and postcard sellers doing particularly good business.

One of the key areas of local trade that prospered due to the increase of so many men in the town's population was the public houses. Not everyone was as happy about this as the publicans. A rather scathing article was published in the *Northampton Independent* on 21 November 1914, which criticised the number of men in khaki that were to be seen on the Wellingborough Road in 'varying stages of intoxication'. It was even suggested that the Licensing Justices of the town were considering closing public houses at 8.30 p.m. However, it should be noted that thirty or so men being drunk on a Friday night out of a total of over 20,000 soldiers could not be considered to represent the majority.

Of the 20,000 soldiers, it was estimated that at least half of them were billeted in local households. Many householders enjoyed the company of the soldiers staying with them as

A photograph of the Bullock family and the soldiers billeted in their house.

The Welsh Fusiliers arriving in Northampton in 1914.

photographs taken with the billeted men testify. However, not everyone was keen to have soldiers staying in their home. What would have been more welcome was the 9*d* a night that was received as compensation for billeting a soldier. Those townsfolk who had stables could expect to receive a further 2*s*, and 7½*d* per day if they provided 10lb of oats, 12lb of hay and 8lb of straw per day per horse stabled with them. A sum of 3*s* would be received for the billeting of officers.

The Welsh Division was not the only division to be billeted in Northampton during the Great War but, perhaps as they were the first, they left an enduring legacy that many local people never forgot. Nor was it forgotten in Wales, and the local papers were filled with letters from appreciative Welsh women who had written to express their thanks to the town for looking after their husbands and sons so well. Mrs Lloyd George (wife of David Lloyd George) was one of those who expressed their thanks, saying, 'The kind hearted hospitality Northampton extended to soldiers from Wales who were billeted here, including my two sons, has greatly endeared the town to Welsh people.'

Special Constables

With so many young able-bodied men away in the army, the police were left short of manpower. A force of Special Constables was much in demand and, in a short period of time, 250 men came forward to fill the void. The men of this force came from all trades and backgrounds. Their work was often long and unrewarding. Many townsfolk regarded them as being officious, especially in enforcing regulations set out by DORA.

As well as keeping the peace, the Special Constables were expected to have knowledge of first aid and be able to perform drill. Their work often carried on into the night and the early hours of the morning, particularly during air raids. In addition to these duties they were also involved in charitable work. Through their own fund-raising they were able to purchase a covered motor car that they used to ferry weary soldiers who had arrived at Northampton's stations during the night to their homes. Without this motor car the soldiers would have faced an overnight stay in Northampton before embarking upon their journey home the next morning. This taxi duty was undertaken by Special Constables who would not finish a shift until the early hours of the morning.

A map contained within a Special Constable's beat book.

Post at St. Edmunds Box.   **BEAT .1.** 2. Hours.

Boundary of Beat.   South side of wellingborough Road,
Lutterworth Road, Billing Road, Alfred Street and St. Edmunds
Street to Post.

        Down St. Edmunds Street, covering
Stockley Street to Billing Road, down Billing Road to
Palmerston Road and return to Vernon Terrace, through
Vernon Terrace and Vernon Street covering Stockley Street
to Wellingborough Road (30 minutes); up Wellingborough Road
to West Street, through West Street to South Street, Along
South Street to Lower Thrift Street, through Lower Thrift
Street to Billing Road covering backways, Billing Road to
Vernon Terrace and return to Cemetery Gates, to Upper Thrift
Street (1 hour); through upper Thrift Street (covering
backways) to South Street, through South Street, South Terrace
Wilby Street to Wellingborough Road, up Wellingborough Road to
Collins Street, (1 hour 15 minutes); down Barry Road to
Billing Road, along Billing Road to Lutterworth Road, up
Lutterworth Road to Wellingborough Road, (1 hour 30 minutes);
along Wellingborough Road to East Street, through East Street
to South Street and through Melbourne Street to Wellingborough
Road, catching shops to New Town Road, (1½ hours); through
New Town Road to South Street, back through Bouverie Street to
Wellingborough Road, down Wellingborough Road to Post.
(2 Hours).

                On this Beat the important property is
shops on the Wellingborough Road, Factories in Barry Road,
Lutterworth Road, Thrift Street, South Street and Stockley
Street.

        END OF BEAT 1.

Beat 1 of the beat book covered the Wellingborough Road area. Important areas to watch were listed as: shops on Wellingborough Road, factories on Barry Road, Lutterworth Road, Thrift Street, South Street and Stockley Street.

                On this Beat the important property is
scattered about.   Special attention should be paid to the
lock-up shops in Abington Square, Wellingborough and
Kettering Road.   Also attention to the Factories in St.
Edmunds Road, Victoria Road, Edith Street, Ethel Street,
Palmerston Road and Pytchley Street.

        2 Beat - 2 Hours.

Post at General Hospital Corner.   Parade at Town Hall.

Boundary of Beat.   Palmerston Road, Billing Road, York
Road, Abington Square, Kettering Road and Exeter Road to Post.

                Up York Road to Abington Square, Abington
Square to St. Edmunds Terrace, (Covering backways of Yards the
florist) (15 minutes); Wellingborough Road to Victoria Road,
Victoria Road to St. Edmunds Road, right of St. Edmunds Road to
York Road, return to Alexandra Road down Alexandra Road to
Billing Road, (30 minutes); along Billing Road to Denmark
Road, up Denmark Road to St. Edmunds Road along St. Edmunds
Road to Pytchley, down Pytchley Street to Thenford Street,

        · (2 Beat) (Continued.)

        Thenford Street in and out , up Pytchley Street to Harold
Street, along Harold Street to Victoria Road, (45 minutes);
left of Victoria Road to Boton Street, through Boton Street
to Pytchley Street, up Pytchley Street to St. Edmunds Road
along St. Edmunds Road to Victoria Road, down Victoria Road
to Billing Road, (1 hour); along Billing Road to Cyril Street
up Cyril Street to St. Edmunds Road, St. Edmunds Road to
Victoria Road, up to Wellingborough Road, to Abington Square,
right hand side of Kettering Road, to Raglan Street, Raglan
Street in and out, (1½ hours); along right hand side of
Kettering Road, through Cleveland Road, Cleveland Road in and
out, Kettering Road to Exeter Road, down Exeter Road to
Wellingborough Road, along Wellingborough Road to Victoria
Road to Wilberforce Street, (1½ hours); Wilberforce Street
in and out, along Wellingborough Road to Palmerston Road,
down Palmerston Road to St. Edmunds Road, along St. Edmunds
Road to Cyril Street, return along St. Edmunds Road to Edith
Street, down Edith Street along Woodford Street to Ethel Street
up Ethel Street to St. Edmunds Road, along St. Edmunds Road
to Palmerston Road, both sides of Palmerston Road to Woodford
Street, (1½ hours); Woodford Street in and out, down
Palmerston Road to Billing Road, Billing Road to Post.(2 hours).

A Special Constable's beat book detailed the limits of each beat. They were numbered sequentially to ensure that each constable was sticking to his designated 'patch'.

Securing the Home Front:
Northampton Citizen Corps

The Northampton Citizen Corps was formed in November 1914 as part of a wider national movement. The corps trained men who were unable to join the regular force – due to their advanced age or other concerns – and taught them musketry, drill and other elementary military skills. After an appeal in the *Northampton Independent* and a subsequent meeting held at the Town Hall, 1,000 men came forward to volunteer. These men joined in order to protect their town in the event of a German invasion and to guard its vital installations against sabotage attacks from enemy agents. Initially, this volunteer military force was completely unsanctioned by the military authorities. No uniforms, weapons or equipment were provided except out of the corps' own funds. Eventually, however, after much lobbying, the authorities officially recognised the corps and their name changed to the Northampton Volunteer Training Corps. By 1916 they had been given full military status as a volunteer force and came directly under the control of the War Office. Officers were given commissions and the men finally received government-issued equipment and training. The cause was also helped when the town's tribunals listed service in the Volunteer Training Corps as a requirement for a man's exemption from regular military service. This influx of men enabled it to grow from one battalion to two. By the end of the war, there were 285,000 volunteers nationwide. Some 101,000 of those men had been ordered to serve as a condition of a tribunal granting an exemption from regular military service.

Lord French, Commander in Chief of Home Forces, reviewed the Northamptonshire Volunteers on 19 November 1916. The force on parade consisted of three battalions, which comprised of 3,140 men from across the county and included the Northampton Citizen Corps. Their smartness and general military bearing was noted and commented upon by Lord French, who is quoted as saying: 'I think it is [a] most satisfactory and encouraging sight to see so fine a body of men at this parade.'

The Northampton Citizen Corps was formed to protect the town whilst the majority of its men were away fighting.

Belgian Refugees

Right from the start of the war, Northampton gave homes to Belgian refugees. These refugees had been either forcibly evicted from their homes by the Germans or had chosen to leave in the wake of the German troops surging through their country. The problem with housing Belgian refugees was that there was no official financial reparations system in place, as there was with the billeting of troops. Nevertheless, many individuals and organisations came forward and provided help and support for the Belgians. An appeal fund was set

TOWN HALL, NORTHAMPTON

Tea & Entertainment

FOR BELGIAN REFUGEES

AT THE INVITATION OF THE MAYOR AND
MAYORESS AND THE BELGIAN
RELIEF COMMITTEE.

TO BE HELD ON
FRIDAY, JANUARY 1st, 1915

'Tea and Entertainment.' The Belgium refugees were made to feel as welcome as possible when they reached Northampton.

up in October 1914 and within a few weeks had raised £74 16s 1d. This fund would raise enough money to pay for 5–8s per week for the billeting of each Belgian refugee. Many local people came forward and offered their homes to the poor Belgians. Mr R. Finnegan placed a large house at their disposal on Colwyn Road whilst Mr Rawlinson, of the Colwyn Road Laundry, carried out all of their washing free of charge.

Some Belgians were luckier in their accommodation than others. The Marquis of Northampton, who at the time was serving with his regiment at the front, sent word to his agent to accommodate some of them at his estate at Castle Ashby. The women and children were billeted in the castle whilst the men were billeted in the armoury. Over the course of the war, many local people took Belgian families into their home to fulfil their patriotic duty and support the war effort. To many the Belgian refugees were a visible reminder of what the country was fighting for. At times the 'demand' to house Belgian refugees even outstripped 'supply'.

Not all of the Belgians that came to Northampton stayed for a prolonged period. Many were only in the town for a very short time, often as little as thirty minutes, whilst their trains took on coal and water on their way to places such as Glasgow. This did not stop many local people from offering their support. Groups of Belgians disembarked at the station and were met by 'kindly-hearted ladies' who gave them coffee, buns and sweets.

By the end of the war over 250,000 Belgian refugees had come to Great Britain. It was the largest-ever influx of refugees in the history of the country. At the end of the war the government offered them free return travel to their native land and in less than twelve months, 90 per cent of the refugees had returned to Belgium.

THE BAKERS OF THE TOWN

The town's bakers proved that it was not always necessary to wear khaki in order to support the war effort. At the start of the war, when the Welsh Division was stationed in the town, the Northampton Co-operative Society was asked to bake bread for the troops. The town's bakers were able to process up to 25 tons of bread a week, in addition to their regular orders. When the division moved to Cambridge the society was asked to continue to supply the baking but the transportation problems proved too much to overcome.

Military Establishments

During the Great War, Northampton had a range of different
military establishments in and around the town, some temporary and some permanent. The increase in the number of men
needed to fight a large-scale modern war meant that the British
Army not only needed to expand the number of troops within
its ranks but also needed to increase its number of training facilities and depots. In addition to the permanent barracks in town,
temporary accommodation was provided at the Racecourse for
both men and horses. Temporary training areas were created in
the town's parks and surrounding fields, and military establishments could be found at the following locations:

*A schematic of
a barrack block.
This was one of
several buildings
that made up
Northampton's
Depot Barracks.*

Northampton Barracks

The Northamptonshire Regiment's Depot Barracks was located
on Barrack Road. The barracks were made up of a number
of buildings constructed in a rectangular shape around the

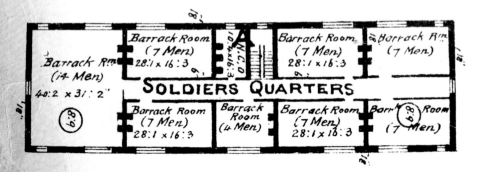

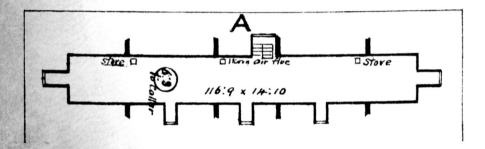

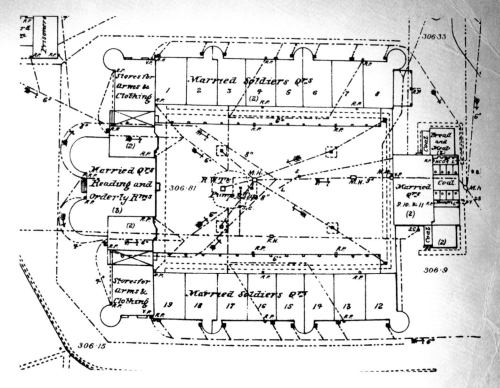

A schematic of the Territorial Headquarters, also known as the Drill Hall.

regimental parade square. They were designed to accommodate one field officer, five officers and 258 privates, NCOs and warrant officers, as well as five horses. They also had a small hospital that could house twenty-six patients, with an isolation unit for two infectious patients. The barrack's magazine had the capacity for 175,000 rounds of rifle ammunition. It also had a tailor's shop, a cobbler's shop, allotment gardens, a guardroom and a recruiting office. The 1911 census recorded that the barracks was home to 235 soldiers. The limited capacity of the barracks explains why those who attested at the start of war were sent home until trains could be arranged to transport them to the regimental camp at Shorncliffe. In short, war had changed. The number of men needed to fight an enemy like Germany – which possessed a larger army – outstripped the British Army's capacity to house soldiers to a pre-war standard.

BE PREPARED
Northampton's Boy Scouts fulfilled the Scout promise to do their 'duty for God and the King' by volunteering their time in aid of the war effort. They helped during air-raid warnings, acted as orderlies in hospitals and barracks, as well as helping to guide new troops to their billets.

The Drill Hall

The Territorial Headquarters, also known as the Drill Hall or Militia Barracks, was located on Clare Street. It was the home to the 4th Battalion of the Northamptonshire Regiment. The Drill Hall was far smaller than Northampton Barracks due to only being designed to accommodate the part-time soldiers of the newly formed Territorial Army, which trained mainly at weekends. The Drill Hall, like the main depot barracks, did contain accommodation for soldiers as well as accommodation for twenty-three married soldiers and their families. It also had stabling for four horses, allotment gardens and a parade square. The Drill Hall's magazine had the capacity for 350,000 rounds of rifle ammunition.

The Drill Hall, 4th (Territorial) Battalion, Northamptonshire Regimental Headquarters.

A picture postcard depicting the Parade Square at Weedon Depot.

Weedon Depot

Just above the village of Lower Weedon is Weedon Depot. As well as being an ordnance depot, Weedon also had a barracks. The site dates back to approximately 1803 and was built when Britain was fighting in another great European war, though in that period France was the enemy. The depot consisted of a series of magazines and storehouses that were located on either side of the canal to enable supplies to be easily unloaded from barges. The depot still stands today but the barracks, which were located near to the Coventry Road, has long since gone. As well as an ordnance store, there were a series of buildings dedicated to the storage of uniform. It was also home to a cavalry barracks and a riding school. The 1911 census recorded 244 soldiers being billeted at Weedon Depot.

The Racecourse

The Racecourse was used extensively by the military during the First World War. It was very quickly turned from a place of recreation and leisure into a vast military encampment consisting of temporary buildings, stables and piles of hay and fodder for the horses. The horses were kept on the Racecourse along with wagons and field guns. The large number of horses and

Troops billeted on the Racecourse. The White Elephant can be seen in the background.

heavy equipment soon took its toll on the previously well-kept site. Before long the ground was churned up into a muddy morass and complaints regarding the damaging of the town's much-loved place of recreation soon reached the local papers. It was also claimed that diseased horses being treated on the Racecourse left behind an infectious disease that spread to the local inhabitants. Many local people, well into the post-war years, claimed to have suffered from 'Racecourse throat'.

Other local parks and recreational grounds were also used by the army. Leonard John Stagg, of the Royal Army Medical Corps, recalled using Abington Park as a training ground. He was a part of a training exercise that involved being placed in a ditch with a note attached to his tunic declaring that he had a broken femur bone. The rest of his section then had to practise carrying him safely over a series of fences and other obstacles, much to the amusement of local civilians.

The Welsh Fusiliers' gun park on the Racecourse.

The 2nd Cheshire Battery on Church Parade at the Racecourse.

3

WORK OF WAR

During the First World War 70 million pairs of army boots were manufactured in the United Kingdom. Just fewer than 50 million of them were produced in Northamptonshire.

The First World War was a total war. This meant that the line between combatants and non-combatants became blurred and those who worked in factories, producing vital products for the war effort, soon became as important a tool for victory as those who served in the military. On the home front, the need to increase the volume of war production drew more and more people, especially women, into the factories. Northampton's key industrial contribution to the war effort was in the production of military boots. Unlike most other towns, Northampton did not have to dramatically retool its factories in order to contribute to the war effort as the town's boot and shoe trade already produced boots for the army and the navy. The main difficulty was to ensure that it retained enough skilled workers to ensure that it could deliver its vital orders. As well as the production of boots for the army and navy, Northampton also contributed in a range of other industrial areas as well as contributing to the important job of nursing wounded servicemen.

APPEAL FOR CHILDCARE
An appeal for public subscriptions to fund day nurseries for working mothers was launched in January 1918. It was hoped that provision of such nurseries would increase the number of women available for vital war work. A sum of £1,000 was needed by the Northampton Corporation. The proposed fee for the care of a child, plus three meals a day, was 9d a day.

Shoe Factories go to War

Northampton has been making shoes wholesale since at least the 1640s. The war with revolutionary France in 1793 meant a dramatic increase in boot production in the town, with 8,000 pairs of shoes being produced per week during this boom time. In many ways, this was the cornerstone of the future prosperity of shoe manufacturing in Northampton with the immediate military need resulting in increased production. The First World War had a similar impact on the town and trade was boosted during what had been a period of slow decline. This decline had resulted from cheaper American imports, which had affected the domestic market from the 1880s onwards. By 1912, however, many of Northampton's larger factories had completed a period of redevelopment and modernisation in order to put them on a par with the modern American factories. The smaller independent shoemakers and outworkers that still existed in Northampton continued to produce between six and seven pairs of shoes a week. This traditional way of working producing high-end results but could not keep up with the new mechanised method of production.

In 1911 the town's population was 90,064; of that number 16,961 people were involved, in one way or another, in the boot and shoe trade. The census of 1911 recorded a staggering twenty-seven differing sub-trades within the boot and shoe industry. These ranged from 'Last Maker' to 'Riveter' from 'Clicker' to 'Boot Binder'. Most factories had employed women before the war but only in a limited number of trades and mostly in the cleaner confines of the closing rooms. As the war progressed and trained manpower dwindled, women soon became employed in a wider variety of trades. They went on to prove that they were capable of doing more than the 'light work' of sewing in the closing rooms. By the end of

OFFICERS' BOOTS
Veldtschoen was a type of waterproof boot that came from the British Army's time in South Africa during the Boer War. The Veldtschoen were designed to keep out ticks but it was found that they were also waterproof. As a result, young officers, with the money to purchase such luxuries, could buy a pair for themselves from Bostocks boot manufacturers and then have them posted out to the Western Front. These high-quality waterproof boots became known as 'officers' boots' as a result. Ordinary infantrymen had to cope with the standard issue Derby pattern boots.

A standard issue boot as produced in Northampton in 1918.

the war, women were doing many of the roles that had only ever previously been done by men.

As well as a boom in the number of pairs of shoes produced, the war also increased the number of manufacturers. In 1911 the town had fifty manufacturers but by 1914 this number had risen to eighty-two. The rest of the county could boast another 184 manufacturers. These factories produced an estimated 50 million pairs of boots during the war, not just for the British Army but also for France, Russia, Italy and other allies. Each nation's needs were slightly different and, as a result, the shoe factories faced many challenges in producing the vast range of boots needed for a variety of climates. Factories produced everything from Italian mountain boots to cold-weather boots for pilots. The difficulties brought about by such large and complicated orders from foreign militaries was exacerbated by the fact that the orders came about during a time when conscription was introduced and some of the factories' most competent men were being called up to serve with the colours. Despite such challenges, the industry managed to adapt and fulfilled its vital war orders.

The war brought a new era of prosperity to the shoe factories; though it must be said that not all factories enjoyed the same level of success. By 1921 the number of factories in the town had fallen back down to fifty-four. The following table shows how some of the most well-known and successful factories fared during the war.

Factory	Production in 1911 (pairs per week)	Production in 1923 (pairs per week)
Crick and Co.	2,000	3,000
Crocket and Jones	12,180	15,000
J. Sear and Co.	11,500	24,000
Church and Co.	4,950	7,000

Wartime Boot Scheme

Northampton's boots equipped not just the British military but other Allied nations. The quality of Northampton's boots was well known worldwide.

Inflation was one of the greatest worries during the First World War and the cost of all goods steadily rose throughout the four years of war. At a time when leather was in short supply and increasing production costs was causing the price of boots and shoes to rise, the War Office decided to step in and institute the wartime Boot Scheme. This scheme was introduced in 1917 in order to ensure that certain standard lines of boots and shoes, particularly suitable for the artisan classes and of medium-grade

Hobnailed boots were hard-wearing and well made. Each manufacturer had their own pattern and designs for the soles of their boots.

quality, were available at fixed prices. This guaranteed that an essential product was being produced at a fair price and that manufacturers and retailers were unable to make large profits by unfairly raising prices.

The essential features of the scheme were:

1 Manufacturers' and distributors' prices should be controlled.
2 The price of boots and shoes should be stamped on the soles of the shoes in order to stop retailers raising the prices.
3 That the boots and shoes should be free from all adulterants.

The scheme was welcomed by the public and over 25 million pairs were made. The scheme went on all the way until April 1919 when the War Office gave up control of civilian footwear.

Bassett Lowke Ltd

Wenman Joseph Bassett Lowke was the founder of Bassett Lowke Ltd. Prior to 1914 the company produced a variety of models but were most famous for the high quality of their model trains. When the war broke out the market for model trains rapidly declined and for the duration of the war Bassett Lowke's production would become dedicated to fulfilling government orders. A large part of the business started to produce 'waterline models' for the Royal Navy with accurate representations of all known ships of the British and German fleet being produced. The British ships were usually modelled in wood and the German ones in metal. These models were then used by the navy to train its personnel in ship identification. Their other government contract was for 'master gauges' that were used in the munitions industry to test all other gauges. This ensured accuracy of machining between factories. The need for such gauges was a product of the Shell Crisis of 1915. This national scandal highlighted that not only was Britain not producing enough shells for the army but that some shells were of an inferior quality. The problem, very simply, was that the quality of shell production was not good enough. Many of the firms that went into munitions production had no previous experience in producing munitions and many of their experienced male machinists had joined up.

What is also interesting about Bassett Lowke is the remodelling of his now famous home at No. 78 Derngate. Constructed in 1815 by William Mobbs, the great-grandfather of Edgar Mobbs, the house was brought for Bassett Lowke by his father in 1916. At the time it was a very standard terraced town house but Bassett Lowke was a forward-thinking man and extremely interested in modern design and architecture. For this reason he enlisted the

No. 78 Derngate today.

help of Charles Rennie Mackintosh in the remodelling of No. 78 Derngate. It is the only house that Mackintosh ever designed. The purchasing and remodelling of the house shows that life still went on during the war. Those with money were still able to provide themselves with a high standard of living.

Bassett Lowke also had connections in Germany and did a lot of business there before the war. This was widely known and, after various accusations, he had to publicly state in his 1916 catalogue that, 'We are distinctly an all British firm- British capital- British directors- British staff- British workmen …' What he did not perhaps state so publicly at the time was that some of his German contacts were interned on the Isle of Man and that he would go and visit them. Also, a lot of the furniture in No. 78 Derngate was produced by internees on the Isle of Man and then shipped over.

Smith, Major & Stevens Ltd

Smith, Major & Stevens Ltd moved from London to Abbey Works, now the site of the Express Lift Tower, in 1909. The company originally produced lifts under the maxim of 'Reliability, Simplicity and Economy' but with the outbreak of war they changed to manufacturing essential items for the war effort. Their previous field of expertise meant that they were perfectly placed to produce winches for the army and navy. These winches were used by the navy to place sea mines on the seabed and by the army to raise and lower observation balloons on the Western Front. The company's lathes were also retooled in order to produce 6-inch howitzer shells for the army and the workshop was specially redesigned to allow for the majority of the production to be carried out by women. A series of ramps, tracks and other ergonomic features were installed in order to reduce the frequency that the heavy shells needed lifting. Perhaps the most unusual aspect of the company's war effort was the production of wheelbarrows for the British and American Army. Although it seems like an unusual requirement for the military, the need for a vast number of wheelbarrows was due to the amount of earth that was excavated each day to create new trenches. This need was met by Smith, Major & Stevens to the tune of around 800 barrows per week, with 17,500 being produced in total.

Caring for the Injured

The large-scale and industrial nature of the war meant that more men were killed and injured at a greater rate than ever before. In order to fight the war effectively, it was not just the army and navy that needed to expand but also their support elements. With an insufficient number of military hospitals and with no national health service, the responsibility for providing care for the injured fell to local hospitals around the country. Northampton was no exception. On 11 August 1914, Northampton Hospital offered fifty beds for injured soldiers.

WREN'S POLISH
William Wren and Company operated out of No. 31 Greyfriars Street. They produced a range of cleaning and polishing pastes and creams for leather products. Their creams were employed by the army for a range of different uses. One vital product that they produced was Wren's Saddle Harness Cream. It was used to help maintain the tack of the army's 1 million horses.

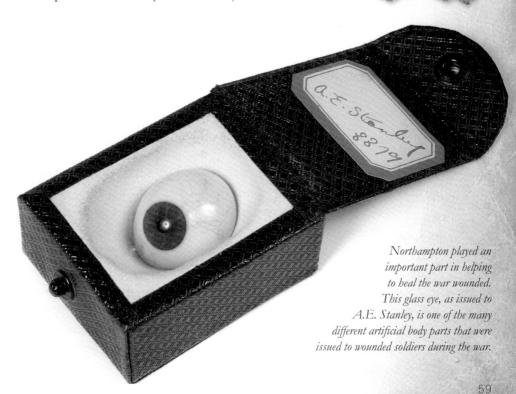

Northampton played an important part in helping to heal the war wounded. This glass eye, as issued to A.E. Stanley, is one of the many different artificial body parts that were issued to wounded soldiers during the war.

Recuperating soldiers, in their hospital blues, pose for a staged photograph in the recreation room at Northampton General Hospital. Before the war the room was used as the boardroom.

The beds were not kept vacant but were made available as and when they were needed.

By 6 February 1915, 117 soldiers had been admitted to the wards. In order to meet the new demand for beds the men had been put in the women's ward and the women had been transferred into the children's wards. By April it was becoming apparent that this solution would not be good enough to meet the growing number of wounded soldiers. As a result, it was decided to erect a wooden pavilion, at a cost of £600, in order to house more soldiers. The pavilion would include accommodation for thirty-two beds, bathrooms, a laundry, an examination room and a sterilising room. The first pavilion was closely followed by a second. The costs for these new buildings were not covered by the military or by the government but by local charitable contributions, with the Red Cross offering to pay £750 to help cover the expense. The hospital's annual

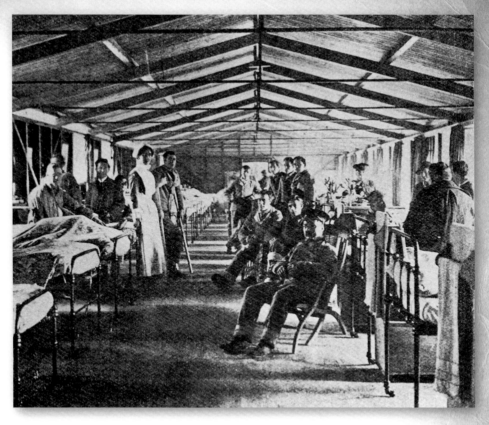

report in 1917 stated that it cost £7 and 6*d* per patient treated against £6 6*s* 7*d* the previous year. Not only was the cost of treating the patients high but, due to inflation, the costs were rising year upon year. In order to cover the expense a series of fund-raising events were held. Several agricultural jumble sales and war bazaars were held and charitable contributions were made by various organisations, including the Red Cross, Northampton Boat Manufacture Association and Messrs Crockett and Jones who contributed £384 towards equipment. In addition to providing beds for the soldiers, the hospital also created a recreation room. The hospital gave up its boardroom in order to give the soldiers the best room in the hospital and put down a lino floor to protect the decorative wooden flooring from the soldiers' hobnail boots. Their plan did not work out as envisaged, however, as the lino stopped the air circulating, causing the floorboards to rot to the extent that

These wounded soldiers are seen in the first temporary pavilion that was erected at Northampton General Hospital.

they needed to be replaced. The boardroom was fitted out with tables, easy chairs, games and even a billiards table. These items were supplied by the owner of a shoe firm in the town who at the time of donation wished to remain anonymous.

On 28 February 1919 the last wounded soldier was discharged and the hospital returned to its pre-war state.

Duston War Hospital and VADs

The vast number of soldiers requiring treatment meant that the hospital alone could not meet the demand. As a result, various other locations round the town were transformed into temporary hospitals for the duration of the war. These Voluntary Aid Detachment (VAD) establishments were dotted in and around the town and were established in a range of different buildings. Even schools, such as Barry Road and Abington Avenue Schools, were converted into small-scale hospitals. The VAD hospitals were established to provide care for wounded soldiers who were not fit enough to return to active service. The VAD nurses would care for the soldiers

A picture postcard of ward 5 at Duston War Hospital.

Ward 5. War Hospital, Duston.

by carrying out duties such as re-bandaging wounds. They also provided a more holistic approach to recovery by putting on entertainment and games for the soldiers.

The largest of them all was established at Berrywood Asylum, which was then renamed Duston War Hospital. Berrywood was established in 1876 as a county asylum and continued in this capacity during the early years of the war, taking on additional patients from other asylums around the country that were being converted into war hospitals. The extra burden of the increased number of patients was accepted by the staff as their way of helping the war effort. The Hospital Committee officially praised the staff for 'the way in which they cheerfully and willingly discharged the extra duties thrown upon their depleted numbers'.

In 1915 it was indicated by the authorities that another hospital in the Midlands was urgently needed in order to increase the number of beds for convalescing soldiers. The Hospital Committee stated:

> ... it to be their duty and their pleasure to place Berrywood and their services at the disposal of the War Office, on the condition that the county suffered no financial loss and that patients were properly provided for. Patients were to be dispersed to other institutions within easy reach ...

By 1916 the transfer from civilian to military hospital had taken place. Additional staff in the form of VAD nurses had been brought in to bolster the number of existing staff. In the two years and ten months between 1916 and 1919 the war hospital cared for 25,000 convalescing soldiers; the last of whom was discharged on 22 March 1919.

SATURDAY WORKING
Before the war a half-day on Saturday was common in many shoe factories but in order to keep up with demand and to make up for the shortfall in trained operatives many factories soon went over to full working days on Saturdays.

SISTER DOLLY

Sister Dolly was one of the many nurses who worked at Duston War Hospital, caring for the convalescing soldiers. Whilst stationed at Duston, Dolly kept an autograph book that was added to by the many soldiers that she came into contact with as part of her daily work. The pages are filled with notes, pictures and poems penned by soldiers from all across the world. Names of men appear from countries all over the Empire: Canada, Australia, South Africa and many more. Some of the verses are short and humorous whilst others are longer and more poignant. One short, and rather flirtatious, verse was written by Rifleman Elliott of the 6th London Regiment:

> Dolly is your name,
> Single is your station,
> Happy to be the gentleman,
> That makes the alteration.

Private Hinscliffe, of the 29th Battalion Canadian Expeditionary Force, added two drawings to the autograph book. One depicts the problems faced in the trenches from rats and the other depicts a Canadian Indian. The autograph book was kept by Sister Dolly as a reminder of the men that she helped to nurse back to health. In addition to this book, a number of picture postcards depicting the inside of the wards have also survived. Reading the comments on the back of the postcards, it is clear how well all of the soldiers felt they were being treated by the staff. These comments, along with the clean and smart-looking wards pictured on the postcard, are a fitting tribute to the fantastic work carried out by all of the nurses in Northampton's wartime hospitals.

"An interrupted Sleep on the Western Front."

Pictorial entry from
Sister 'Dolly' Derham's autograph book.

Working-class Grievances

In May 1917 a series of strikes took place in the town. The grievances of the workers were varied but the commissioners for Yorkshire and the East Midlands found that food prices and profiteering were the basic grievances. When the rate of inflation is considered, these grievances can be well understood. A quart of milk in 1914 would cost an average of 3½*d* but by 1917 this had risen to 7½*d*. Other issues included conscription, pay, the dilution of skilled labour and poor housing. For instance, a good heel trimmer could produce 1,150 heels per day whereas new unskilled workers could only produce 750 per day. The discontentment that was felt by the trained artisans about the dilution of their skilled professions is easy to understand. But not everyone at the time could see both sides of the argument. *Northampton Independent*'s Jupiter, always forthright in his views, contrasted forty operatives who went on strike at Church and Co.'s shoe factory in 1916 with wounded and dying soldiers in Northampton Hospital and declared a momentary longing for a 'dictator of the Cromwell type' and for some form of martial law to stop such events.

Another example of the workers' grievances is with the rate of pay for Saturday working. Most factories worked half a day on Saturday even before the war. As the war progressed and production needed to be increased, the workers were asked to put in full days on Saturdays. Many employees felt that they should be paid an additional amount, on top of their standard pay, for doing overtime on a Saturday. The factory owners believed that their employees were being greedy and in return the workers felt that the 'shoe barons' were trying to profiteer out of the war.

Women at War

With so many young men answering their country's call, there was a manpower shortage in many key industries. Nationally this shortage became apparent during the 'shell scandal' of 1915.

In Northampton the impact was felt most in the shortfall of manpower in the boot and shoe industry. This manpower shortage was a vicious circle: not only did shoe trade workers leaving the factories for the forces create a shortfall in trained employees but they themselves increased the number of military boots that were required. The industry did not turn immediately to women; men who were unemployed were called in first. But as the war progressed and the demand for boots increased, the shoe factory owners realised that they would have to turn to female operatives.

Nationally, the total number of women in paid employment increased from 5,966,000 in July 1914 to 7,311,000 in July 1918, which is an increase of 1,345,000. Of most importance is not the increase in the number of women who went into work

More and more women entered the shoe trade during the war.

but the change in the nature of the work that women undertook. Many women had worked before the start of the war but for many women this only meant part-time or seasonal work, such as helping with the harvest. The First World War gave many women the chance to work full time and in a diverse range of occupations. Working-class women took jobs in industry, such as working in munitions factories or in the shoe trade. Middle and upper-class women, meanwhile, had a wider range of options available to them. For instance, they could join organisations such as the First Aid Nursing Yeomanry. Women who joined the First Aid Nursing Yeomanry and the Voluntary Aid Detachments were expected to do so at their own expense and had to purchase their own uniforms. By 1918 over 1,000 women from Northamptonshire had volunteered to be a VAD, serving either at home or abroad. Other, more sedate, roles included clerical and secretarial jobs. This increase in secretarial duties meant that by 1918 women accounted for 47 per cent of the workforce in government establishments.

Although the number of jobs open to women had increased, women were still paid less than men even though they worked the same long hours. Many women worked twelve-hour days for six days a week and, on average, women were paid between 50 and 66 per cent less than their male counterparts. However, as many working-class women had left very low-paying roles, such as domestic service, they were still earning more than before the war. By 1917, 2,400 women were working in agriculture in Northamptonshire. Many of them were trained at the Experimental Farm at Moulton. When fully trained they could earn an average of around 31s 9d per week. Although this change in occupation is significant, it is worth noting that domestic service was still recorded as the most common female occupation in 1918.

Although many women went to work for patriotic reasons, others also went to put bread on the table. With husbands and sons in the forces, many household incomes decreased during the war. This, combined with a very steep rate of annual inflation, left many households short. Wives were entitled to a percentage of their husband's pay, which was deducted automatically, and they would also receive addition funds per each dependant in their household. This could be topped up by money that the husband sent home from the front.

The Old and the Young

Not only were women being called into industry but young people were also benefitting from improved opportunities. The *Northampton Independent* reported on 22 January 1916 that many young people, some as young as 14 or 15, were being paid as much as 18s to £1 a week for simple mechanical operations in local munitions factories. When compared to the money earned by a soldier on the front line, the hard work and long hours in a munitions factory were very well paid. Those serving overseas, however, often resented such high rates of pay. Many people were accused of getting themselves jobs in munitions factories not only for the high wages but because they now believed that this would prevent them from being called up as it was a reserved occupation.

As well as women and children, old men were being called back into the boot trade. Many of these men were in their late sixties and early seventies and hadn't seen the inside of a shoe factory for ten years or more. Although they were not as young as they had once been, they were often preferable to the employment of women as they were seen as skilled craftsmen who had earned their trade. Many of them could have as much work as they desired or could practically handle. They could earn up to £3 per week.

4

News From the Front

You are leaving home to fight for the safety and honour of my Empire.

Belgium, whose country we are pledged to defend, has been attacked and France is about to be invaded by the same powerful foe.

I have implicit confidence in you my soldiers. Duty is your watchword, and I know your duty will be nobly done.

I shall follow your every movement with deepest interest and mark with eager satisfaction your daily progress, indeed your welfare will never be absent from my thoughts.

I pray God to bless you and guard you and bring you back victoriously.

King George V, message to troops, 12 August 1914

Although this book is about the everyday life of the town during the Great War, it would not be complete without mention of the men who left the town to go and fight. This chapter contains information about each battalion of the Northamptonshire Regiment as well as the Northamptonshire Yeomanry. Due to the confines of this chapter, the number of battalions involved and the vast array of battles during the war, only key events have been picked out.

His Majesty the King meeting the 12-year-old Belgian boy who had become the 1st Battalion's regimental mascot.

Life in the Trenches

Private Ron James on no-man's-land:

> In winter No Man's Land was a terrible place to gaze on – a scene of desolation with spectral shell-shattered trees and quagmires awaiting to trap the unwary who ventured out into its terrain. Late spring and summer showed a different aspect entirely with wild flowers blooming, grass and even cultivated crops like wheat covering up the many scars of war. Sometimes even the shell-torn trees burst into life and leaves appeared upon their gaunt frames, whilst skylarks and other songbirds could be heard above the sound of the guns. It was at times like these that No Man's Land presented to the observer a paradox of both savagery and beauty.

The rule of thumb for the construction of a front-line trench was that it should be as deep as the tallest man in the company plus an additional length of approximately the tip of the finger to the elbow. This depth of trench would protect a front-line soldier from anything but a direct hit. Trench warfare was nothing new and trenches had been dug during the American Civil War and during the Crimean War. Their appearance on the battlefields of the Great War was not anticipated by the military leaders of either side, but by 1914 the rise in the number of machine guns and rapid-firing artillery pieces available meant that as soon as the German's great advance into France and Belgium was halted the only way of holding a position without sustaining massive casualties was to dig defence positions. These positions took the form of trenches. This was the situation from the winter of 1914 right through to the late summer of 1918 when the Allies broke out of the trench deadlock during their victorious '100 Days' offensive.

This period between the lines solidifying after the initial German advance and the Allies' 100 Days offensive is referred to as trench warfare. The conditions within the trenches varied greatly depending upon the period that the trenches were constructed, the local geology and the geography of the site, the time of year and the materials available. In addition to these variables, it must also be kept in mind that it was not a single German trench facing a single British trench but a whole series of lines of trenches. Front-line trenches would have support and reserve trenches behind them and soldiers would generally spend around four days in each line of trenches. They would start in the front line and serve for around three to four days and then move back further away from the Germans to the next trench line. This meant that the soldiers got a chance to rest and were not always in the firing line. Of course, even for those in the front-line trenches, sometimes less than 100m away from the enemy, it was not always a case of constant fighting. A soldier's daily life on the front-line trench would often consist of boring daily chores such as emptying the latrine, repairing the trenches and cleaning equipment. Some sectors were known to be quieter and more peaceful than others. After a while the whole battalion would be moved out of the trenches and into an area behind the lines where they could recover, recuperate and conduct training.

Lieutenant Arthur White recalled in a letter home that where possible during bad weather, areas of trenches would be relinquished if their condition was thought to be unsuitable: 'The weather conditions were pretty slippery at first; in some parts we had to abandon them. Men do not stand up to their waist in water out here; it is only in the columns of the *Daily Mail*.'

It must also be remembered that many people never went near the front line. The army needed all of the trades that civilian life relied on and, as a result, men could find themselves working as a baker, a clerk, a wagon driver or a horse groom, or – in the case of some Northamptonshire men – as mobile boot repairers.

Trench Routine

It is difficult to give an exact overview of a typical day in the trenches due to the number of variables that need to be taken into account. Variables such as the weather, standing orders, the particular year of the war, as well as the area of line being held, would affect the daily lives of the soldiers on the front line. One of the most influential factors would be how aggressive the opposing German unit facing that section of line was. For a period of relative quiet a soldier's typical day may well have gone as follows:

06:30

Wake up. The men are woken up to prepare for the break of dawn.

07:00 to 08:00

Stand to. The men would man the firing steps in the trench and prepare themselves for a German attack. Dawn and dusk are the two times of day when attacks are most likely. The men in the trenches stare into the darkness looking for any sign of enemy movement.

08:00

Sunrise.

08:30

Stand down. Men are issued with a rum ration (rum was issued during cold weather and before attacks).

08:30 to 09:00

Breakfast and morning routine. This meal could consist of a range of foodstuffs depending upon the current supplies. Fresh bread, butter, jams and even freshly cooked bacon were a staple. Men would shave and clean themselves.

09:00 to 11:00

Trench duties. The men would carry out the cleaning of their weapons as well as carrying out other daily chores.

11:00 to 12:00

Sleep. The requirement to take turns being on sentry duty in the night (one man in three to be on sentry at any one time) meant that the safer daylight hours were ideal for catching up on sleep. Men could also write letters home and read the local newspapers that were sent to the front line.

12:00

Lunch. Lunch would consist of stew and army biscuits. Army biscuits were so hard that they were normally soaked in tea before the men would attempt to eat them.

13:00 to 14:00

Sentry duty. Fewer sentries were required in the daytime. Men would take it in turns to watch the German lines whilst the others went about their daily business.

14:00 to 15:30

Working parties. Any heavy rain in the night may well have caved in some of the trench walls. Trench repairs and alterations were a vital part of trench life. A soldier would have been as familiar with a spade as with a rifle.

Standing orders dictated the day-to-day routine of soldiers on the front line.

Trench orders for the 1st Battalion Northamptonshire Regiment.

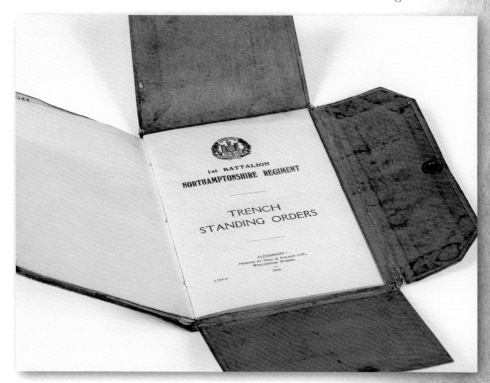

15:30 to 16:30

Preparations and stand to. The men prepare themselves for the setting of the sun and the return of a dangerous period of the day. If the men were required to leave the trench that night to go on a trench raid or patrol then the preparations for these duties would be made at this point. Just like in the morning, the men would be stood to in order to watch the German lines.

16:30

Sunset.

18:00

Supper. Supper would be served to the men.

The time of year would be one of the key factors that affected the daily agenda. The summer was the most preferable time of year to be in the trenches. Obviously, it would be warmer and more pleasant, but most importantly the hours of darkness are shorter. Trench raids and patrols into no-man's-land were carried out at night, which meant that more men needed to be on guard at once, thus long summer days gave soldiers longer periods of peace.

Northamptonshire Regiment

The Northamptonshire Regiment came into being in 1881. It was created by the amalgamation of the 48th (Northamptonshire) Regiment of Foot and the 58th (Rutlandshire) Regiment of Foot. The 48th became the 1st Battalion Northamptonshire Regiment and the 58th became the 2nd Battalion Northamptonshire Regiment.

The regimental cap badge, which was worn on the front of the trench cap, displayed a mixture of symbolic references to these two predecessor regiments. The battle honour Gibraltar and the castle relate to the period that the 58th Regiment spent at the garrison of Gibraltar between 1775 and 1783. The battle honour Talavera and the laurel relates to the 48th Regiment's actions

A Northamptonshire Regiment cap badge. This would have been worn on the front of a field service cap by an enlisted soldier.

A silk cigarette card depicting the Northamptonshire Regiment. Such items were given away with cigarettes during the Great War.

in 1809 at the Battle of Talavera during the Peninsular War. These battle honours, displayed on the cap badge, served to unite the men in a shared *esprit de corps* of their regiment's past honours and glory. The bi-metal badge, which normally comprised of a white metal badge with a brass scroll, was replaced for economy purposes with an all brass badge. This was easier and cheaper to produce for the large number of Kitchener men joining the ranks.

THE NORTHAMPTONSHIRE REGIMENT
48th & 58th Foot.

65   B.D.V. CIGARETTES.

THE BATTLE
OF THE DUNES

On 4 July 1917, after a period of rest and retraining that had brought the battalion back up to full strength, the 1st Battalion Northamptonshire Regiment became one of two units to hold the extreme left flank of the whole Allied line. Their position was between the town of Nieuport and the Channel coast. Along with the 2nd Battalion King's Royal Rifle Corps, the Northamptons occupied a forward position in front of the Yser Canal. This area was described by the Regimental History Committee as 'nothing but sand – flat, as a rule, but with dunes rising some sixty feet above sea level, and thick clusters of rushes to break the monotony'. The sandy soil meant that conventional trenches were out of the question. Instead, breastworks were used to sure up their positions. These positions were easily observed by the enemy and did not provide good cover. To make matters worse, their forward position was the other side of the canal, which meant that they were isolated from the rest of the 1st Division. The only way of crossing the canal was via three 'plank bridges' assembled by the Royal Engineers.

This extreme left flank was generally a very quiet sector, where new officers and section commanders could be put through their paces. As a result of the perceived peacefulness of the sector, more men were left out of the front-line positions than usual and only two out of four company commanders were in the fighting line at any one time.

The decision to limit the number of men in the front lines turned out to be a very fortuitous one as the fighting that transpired on 10 July 1917 heralded one of the darkest days of the Northamptonshire Regiment during the whole war. At around six o'clock a massive German artillery barrage commenced. The bombardment was extremely heavy and many men were to later recall that it was one of the greatest onslaughts that they had ever endured. The British artillery, outnumbered and outgunned by the German artillery, had very little reply and the sandy trenches were no match for such a fierce attack. The Northampton's position soon became nothing but a series of interconnecting shell holes and the three bridges across the canal were destroyed by German fire, leaving no means of escape. When the German bombardment lifted, after twelve hours, the Northamptons were attacked by a Marine Division, which forced its way between them and the King's Royal Rifle Corps. The casualties were extremely high. Luckily, 400 men had been kept back on the other side of the canal, out of the fighting lines, but in total 570 men were killed, wounded or captured. Only nine men managed to escape by swimming the Yser Canal. Seven men escaped by using a rope fastened to a pontoon and another two men swam the river in order to warn nearby units of the German's breakthrough. One of those men was Sergeant Mansfield who was awarded a Distinguished Conduct Medal for his action. The other was Sergeant Cope, who was awarded the Military Medal. Sergeant Cope's matter-of-fact account was later published in the *Northampton Independent*. It reads:

As there was nobody left I retired to the canal, ten of the Germans trying to 'scotch' me, but I only got a tap in the back. I dashed into the canal which was about 40 feet wide, and got safely to the other side though the Germans were still having a 'splosh' at me. I thought that was no place for me, so I got off as quickly as possible. I reached the next division's headquarters, made a report of what the enemy had done as far as I could and then had a lot of 'how do you do' [whisky].

Background image – an artist's impression of the disastrous Battle of the Dunes, taken from The War Illustrated.

1st Battalion Northamptonshire Regiment (the 48th)

On 13 August 1914 the 1st Battalion left Great Britain for the Continent, landing at Le Havre at daybreak on the following morning. They formed part of the British Expeditionary Force (BEF), which was Great Britain's rapid-reaction force, and were attached to the 1st Division, making up part of the 2nd Infantry Brigade. The 1st Battalion was one of the British units to be involved in the now famous 'Retreat from Mons' where the British and French forces were forced back by the advancing Germans to the River Marne, where the German advance was then halted. On the retreat Captain Needham happened upon a brand new Metallurgique motor car in the grounds of a chateau near Givry. He recalled:

> I thought this was too good to leave to the Germans, so I tried hard to start it up, but without success. That being no good, and not having time to make the car un-driveable, I pushed the point of my sword through all four of the tyres and punctured them. Incidentally, this was the only useful piece of work this weapon performed during the whole war.

BATTALION MASCOT
The men of the 1st Battalion Northamptonshire Regiment adopted a 12-year-old Belgian orphan by the name of Joseph Lefeure as their unofficial mascot. The boy would travel around with the battalion's transport section. They even went as far as to clothe him in a miniature army uniform. Apparently, the boy later went on to join a Belgian regimental band.

From the Marne the British and French launched a counter-attack on the Germans and advanced to the River Aisne. Here the 1st Battalion won a name for itself in both local and national newspapers. The Battle of the Aisne resulted in deadlock and, as neither side could advance, they both began 'digging in'. The entrenched positions of both sides were hard to attack from the front so each side carried out a series of outflanking manoeuvres to the north until eventually both sides had reached the sea. This series of actions became known as the 'Race to the Sea'. Thereafter trench warfare became the norm.

2nd Battalion Northamptonshire Regiment (the 58th or the Steelbacks)

The 2nd Battalion was based in Alexandria when the war broke out. On 6 November 1914 they arrived at Le Havre and they were later one of the units involved in the now famous Christmas truce. The battalion's war diary recorded that the men of the 2nd Battalion fraternised with the Germans in no-man's-land on both Christmas Eve and Christmas Day and that soldiers of both sides exchanged souvenirs and cigarettes. Luckily the troops facing them in the trenches on Christmas 1914 were Saxons and not Prussians. The Prussians had a reputation for being the most aggressive of all of the German units and therefore less likely to have been so seasonally cheerful.

The Battle of Aubers Ridge took place on 9 May 1915. It was part of a wider Franco-British effort to break the trench stalemate but it ended in complete disaster. The attack resulted in heavy losses for the British Army with over 11,000 casualties; 986 of them belonged to the Northamptonshire Regiment. Both the 1st and the 2nd Battalions were part of the first wave.

A picture postcard featuring the regimental colours of the 2nd Battalion (58th) Northamptonshire Regiment.

LICE

It was impossible to keep yourself clean. We had lice in our hair, on our bodies, in our boots and even in our tin hats! ... of course, there was little we could do about our unwanted lodgers except keep their numbers down and after a time we got used to them ...

Private Ron James

The 1st Battalion lost 560 men and seventeen officers whilst the 2nd Battalion lost 426 men and twelve officers. The miserable failure of the attack was due to a number of reasons. Primarily, it resulted from a lack of intelligence about the German positions, the absence of a surprise element and an insufficient preliminary bombardment by the artillery. The British Army had a lot to learn about trench warfare and it wasn't until 1918 that it had rectified its deficiencies in both tactical doctrine and weaponry. The lessons that the army learnt in these early years of the war were vitally important but they were lessons that cost a high price.

Sadly, no memorial stands at Aubers Ridge to commemorate the men who lost their lives there.

3rd (Reserve) Battalion Northamptonshire Regiment

Contrary to the myths, the British Army was not made up entirely of young men. Private A.V. Collins, of Lawrence Street, was aged 38 when he was killed in action in 1917.

The 3rd Battalion consisted of what was once the Militia. It was mobilised on 4 August 1914 and, within a day, 832 men of the reserves had presented themselves at the Northampton Depot Barracks. So many arrived in such a short period of time that it was reported that many had to go without blankets and even supper on those first few nights of the war. The 3rd Battalion's role in the war would be to act as a training and reserve unit for the other battalions. They would collect and

Beloved, through a mist of tears,
We two are parted for a space;
I look back through the happy years,
And see again your loving face.

You wended forth, and left me here,
I longed to keep you, all in vain;
But I feel that you are ever near,
And God will join us soon again.

In Loving Memory of

PRIVATE A. V. COLLINS

(Manchester Regiment).

DEARLY LOVED HUSBAND OF ANNIE COLLINS.

19, Lawrence Street, Northampton.

Who was Killed in Action in France,
on October 7th, 1917.

AGED 38 YEARS.

prepare men, ready to dispatch them to whichever battalion needed extra forces to bring themselves back up to strength. As a result of this, 20,000 men would pass through the ranks of the 3rd Battalion. Within a week of the war breaking out, the 3rd Battalion was moved down to Weymouth; by the end of the war they were based in Ireland.

The Northamptons are inspected at the front line.

4th (Territorial) Battalion Northamptonshire Regiment

The 4th Battalion formed part of the Territorial Force; a military entity that came into being as a result of the 1908 army reforms. The new force was designed to replace the Rifle Volunteers. Although not designed to be mobilised for overseas service in the event of war, Territorial soldiers could still volunteer to serve abroad. These men were entitled to

A.77.FIELD BOOT REPAIRERS 4⁺ N⁰ REGT.

4th (Territorial) Battalions boot repairers hard at work.

wear an Imperial Service Badge on the right breast of their tunic. They trained in the evenings after work and also at weekends, leading them to be christened Saturday Night Soldiers. They would also complete an annual camp every summer in order to brush up on their military skills. The 4th Battalion was on one such camp when war was declared.

The men of the Territorial Force were divided into two on 15 August 1914. The 1/4th Battalion was created for those who wished to serve overseas whilst the home service men joined one of two newly created training battalions known as the 2/4th and 3/4th. Unlike the rest of the Northamptonshire Regiment's battalions, the 1/4th Battalion would not serve on the Western Front. They took part in the campaign in the Middle East, which was often referred to by the press at the time as a sideshow. They fought at Gallipoli, Egypt and in Palestine.

5th (Pioneer) Battalion Northamptonshire Regiment

The 5th Battalion was a pioneer battalion. The role of pioneers in the Great War was very varied. They performed a wide range of tasks that could include digging trenches, building gun emplacements, filling sandbags, carrying supplies to the front, burying telephone cables, building duckboards and many more tasks besides. A lot of these tasks would have been carried out at night-time and in close proximity to the front lines. When an attack had gone 'over the top' and the German front-line positions had been captured it would have been the job of the pioneers to come in and connect the newly captured trenches with the pre-existing British lines. Not only was this hard and arduous work but it was also dangerous. German artillery would send shells over and there was also the likelihood of counter-attacks. Pioneers were primarily there to carry out construction tasks but they were also equipped with rifles and took part in the fighting on numerous occasions.

When fresh bread could not be brought to the front-line trenches, soldiers had to put up with Hard Tack biscuits. The biscuits were so hard that they were often used as postcards by the troops.

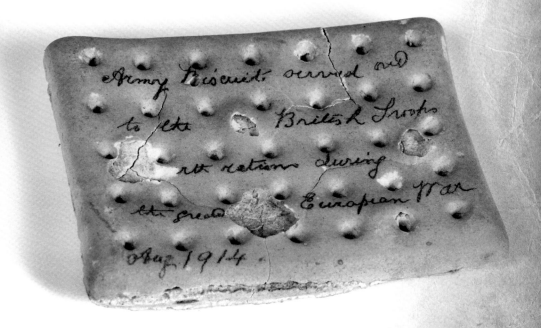

6th (Service) Battalion Northamptonshire Regiment

The men who answered Lord Kitchener's call for volunteers were formed up into service battalions. They were often referred to as the men of Kitchener's Army. The new service battalions were placed within pre-existing infantry regiments. The title 'service' referred to the fact that the battalion was for war service only and would be disbanded after the war. The 6th Battalion was formed in Northampton in September 1914.

After ten months of training, the battalion landed in France on 26 July 1915. Like many battalions of Kitchener's Army, the 6th Battalion would see their first major action on 1 July 1916 at the Battle of the Somme. They took part in the action to take Pommiers Redoubt on the first day of the Somme offensive and on 14 July they were involved in the successful capture of Trones Wood.

7th (Service) Battalion Northamptonshire Regiment

The 7th Battalion, also known as Mobbs' Own, did not have the easiest introduction to army life. Like many other new battalions at the time they were seriously underequipped. In fact when they were dispatched to the coast to undertake training, they arrived to discover that not enough blankets had been provided for the men. In order to quickly rectify the situation, Mobbs wrote to the town's mayor and asked him to provide the men with as many blankets as he could. Within a couple of days the mayor had arranged the collection and dispatch of 260 blankets.

Once the battalion was fully trained and equipped, they departed Great Britain on 31 August 1915. The following month, on 25 September, they received a baptism of fire at the Battle of Loos. This was the first time that the men of Kitchener's Army were put into action. It was also the first time that poisoned gas had been used during an attack. The action at Loos was a failure – only marginal amounts of ground were captured from the Germans and the 7th Battalion alone took 400 casualties (roughly split between half wounded and half killed) of all ranks.

8th (Reserve) Battalion Northamptonshire Regiment

The 8th Battalion was a reserve unit formed at Weymouth in October 1914. It was responsible for training men for the other battalions.

1st and 2nd Garrison Battalion Northamptonshire Regiment

The garrison battalions were second-line units comprised of men who were deemed not fit enough to fight but who were able to play an important role guarding key locations. The 1st Garrison Battalion served in Egypt and Palestine whilst the 2nd Garrison Battalion was a home service unit that spent the war in Great Britain.

Northamptonshire Yeomanry

The Northamptonshire Yeomanry was formed in 1794 as a volunteer cavalry regiment. It became part of the Territorial Force in 1908. Along with the 4th Battalion Northamptonshire Regiment, their headquarters were at the Drill Hall on Clare Street. 'A' squadron was based at Northampton with a detachment at Cottesbrooke, 'B' squadron was based at Peterborough, 'C' squadron was based at Kettering and 'D' squadron was based at Daventry. The men of the yeomanry were good horsemen, many of whom were well known and respected countrymen. Many of the men and their horses were part of the famous Pytchley Hunt.

> **A LUCKY ESCAPE**
> Private H. Hill of the 1st Battalion Northamptonshire Regiment had a lucky escape on 7 November 1914 when his cap badge deflected a German bullet. Hill also received a shrapnel wound to the hand and was rendered unconscious for two days.

The unit mobilised in October 1914 and crossed the Channel on 5 November, disembarking at Le Havre. It joined the 8th Division and fought in the fighting line in the Merville-Estairs sector, where it remained throughout the winter. Much of their time in France was spent on duties that may not have been expected of a cavalry formation. They were called upon to dig trenches, to dispatch messages, carry equipment to the front as well as acting as guides for new units coming to the front. The yeomanry did eventually get the opportunity to put their horsemanship into practice in 1917 when they fought in the Battle of Arras. They had the distinction of becoming the first cavalry unit to enter Arras. By 10 November 1917 the yeomanry had sailed for Italy in order to fight the Austrians. They were involved in the successful campaign that saw the yeoman undertake a traditional cavalry action and capture 1,500 prisoners in the space of two days.

The yeomanry originally consisted of one regiment, which expanded as the war progressed. A second-line regiment was soon formed back in Britain in order to train and equip new reinforcements. This unit, based at Towcester, was created in September 1914 and became known as the 2/1st Northamptonshire Yeomanry. A third-line unit called the 3/1st Northamptonshire Yeomanry was created in 1915 as a training unit and was based at Canterbury.

5

KEEP THE HOME FIRES BURNING

These orders will come into force on January 10th. Every local householder is affected, for the order definitely states that in ... dwelling houses inside lights, back and front, must be so shaded or reduced, or the windows, skylights, and glass doors so screened by shutters or dark blinds and curtains ... that no more than a dull subdued light is visible from any direction outside.

Lighting restrictions, 1 January 1916
Northampton Independent

Military Service Act and the Tribunals

The conscription of men into the armed forces was brought about for the first time in British history in 1916. Exemptions from the Military Services Act could be granted to an individual by a local tribunal. The tribunals could grant exemptions to those who convincingly demonstrated that they met one of four criteria. These criteria were:

- If it is expedient in the national interest that he should be engaged in other work [munitions factories, for example]

- If serious hardship would ensue owing to his exceptional financial or business obligations [if he was the sole bread winner and had dependants to support]
- Ill health or infirmity
- Conscientious objection to the undertaking of combatant service

The exemptions could be either full exemptions from military service or temporary exemptions. The Northamptonshire Tribunal saw 61 per cent of men receive temporary or conditional exemptions. If they had support from their employer then their appeal was more likely to succeed. Very few exemptions on conscientious grounds were given full exemptions; most were given non-combatant duties within the military. The tribunal itself consisted of local noteworthy citizens and military representatives. Northampton was serviced by the Borough Tribunal and if an appeal was made then it would be overseen by the Northamptonshire County Tribunal.

Many of the exemptions that were given were for short periods only, with the typical period of exception being around three months. More than one exemption could be granted and an individual could receive multiple exemptions, one after another. George Williamson, a master baker, was given several exemptions, amounting to a total of one year's deferral. His mother applied for an exemption on his behalf on the grounds that she would come into financial hardship if he was conscripted as she was 75 years old and unable to run the business herself. Probably one of the shortest deferral of military service was Wilfred Whitlock, a milkman, who only received an eleven-day exemption. The two trades most likely to receive exemptions were agriculture (43 per cent) and the shoe industry (31 per cent). The exemption could also be accompanied by caveats such as the requirement to serve in the Northampton Volunteer Training Corps. Those who objected on ethical or religious grounds to combatant service were permitted to serve in non-combat roles, such as driving ambulances in the Royal Army Medical Corps.

The boot and shoe manufacturers of the town were incredibly concerned by the introduction of the Military Services Act. Northamptonshire had no comparison nationally for an industry that was so key to its local economy. Average weekly output of factories in Northampton alone was £150,000 and the manufacturers were worried that their diminished workforce, already struggling with demand, would be further reduced until no trained men were left. They were right to be worried, as the shoe industry did not enjoy the same level of protection as munitions works. In October 1916, James Gribble reported to the tribunal that American orders of £1 million for ladies and children's shoes were unable to be placed in the town due to work for the army. To make matters worse local shops had now started to stock American-produced shoes.

The shoe industry, like agriculture, was made up of a high proportion of men who were considered to be of either A or B1 health (A being the fittest that a man could be). The 'rough stuff' work paid good money but was a rigorous job and required lots of physical labour. Not a lot of women wished to work in such a department. In April 1916 one Northampton factory reported having lost some 200–300 men since the war commenced. The owner of another firm, producing 15,000 pairs of army boots a week in March 1916, stated that of his forty-eight remaining clickers (a predominantly male role), only thirteen were of military age and that several women were now employed in his traditionally male-dominated staff.

As the first Military Service Act came into force, the industry's capacity was being tested further by an order for 6 million pairs of boots for the Russian Army. At roughly the same time, an order was also being placed for the Italian Army. They were both of different designs and required a lot of setting up of machines and new processes.

NORTHAMPTON'S TRIBUNALS

Anyone wishing to contest being conscripted into the army could have their case heard at one of two local tribunals. Men of the town had their case heard at the Northampton Borough Tribunal whilst those in the surrounding villages were covered by the Northampton Rural Tribunal. Any man who was not happy with the tribunal's decision could appeal to the County Tribunal. It must be remembered that although a man could contest a tribunal's decision, so could the army.

The tribunal was very sensitive to the new orders. Many of the tribunal's panel were associated with the trade and could call local experts to express their opinions on the various exemptions that had been applied for. The first public sitting of the tribunal was on 25 February 1916 and it was decided that there would be a three-month period where there would be a blanket exemption for all men working in the boot trade, in order to accommodate the new orders. Captain Wright, Northamptonshire's recruiting officer, agreed not to challenge these exceptions.

In October 1916, new War Office instructions to the military representatives required that they should appeal any exceptions offered to men below 30 years of age regardless of their circumstances. No local agreements were to be allowed or tolerated. This caused Captain Wright to challenge all exceptions for men under the age of 30, even if they were essential for the new orders. In contradiction to these instructions from the War Office, the Ministry of Munitions wrote to the boot manufacturers of Northampton and urged them to retain their workforce. An agreement was eventually reached where some deferrals could be granted whilst orders were still in place.

Some exemptions were applied for due to conscientious objection to war. By March 1916 a branch of the No Conscription Fellowship had been established in response to the Military Services Act and was supporting conscientious objectors in their appeals to the various tribunals. Harold Croft – the secretary of the Northampton Independent Labour Party (ILP), vice-president of the Northampton Labour Representation Committee, member of the executive committee of Northampton Trades Council and a full-time employee of the ILP as its Midlands divisional secretary – supported a number of conscientious objectors who sought to appeal in this way.

By 1916, Croft had received his own call-up papers. He appeared before the Borough Tribunal in July and refused to enlist on conscientious grounds, though not – like most conscientious objectors – on religious grounds. Those who refused to fight were offered alternative service with the

YMCA or other non-combatant roles such as the medical services. Croft, however, completely refused any form of alternative service. The tribunal adjourned for one month to allow him to obtain 'work of national importance'. The case was then escalated to the County Tribunal. Croft believed that his political work with the ILP was of vital national importance but the tribunal was not convinced and nor was the Central Tribunal. On 23 September he received notice to report to the barracks. He returned the notice with a letter stating that he was a conscientious objector and was unable to attend. As a result he was fined £2 by the magistrate and handed over to a military escort. He was then court-martialled for disobeying an order to sign his record of service papers. Croft argued that he was not disobeying orders as he was not a soldier and had taken no oath and signed no military paperwork. He was sentenced to six months' hard labour, then followed a further sentence of 112 days' hard labour, which was immediately followed by another court martial. The final court martial sentenced him to two years' imprisonment.

Public opinion regarding those who appealed to the tribunals is hard to gauge. Jupiter, in his weekly editorial in the *Northampton Independent*, often criticized those who he believed were falsely hiding behind exemptions and who were not prepared to do their duty. Not everyone in the town felt the same. Some people, including Malcolm Ernest Hancock, who served as an officer in the Northampton Regiment, felt sorry for those who were true conscientious objectors and felt that they had a 'hard time of it'.

Charitable Contributions

At the outbreak of war many people in Great Britain believed that the conflict would be over by Christmas 1914. When this predication did not come to fruition various morale-boosting exercises were introduced both at home and at the front. One of the most popular campaigns was the Princess Mary

Christmas Fund. The national fund provided men on active service with an embossed brass tin that contained a selection of photographs, tobacco, cigarettes and a pipe. There was also an alternative of sweets and chocolate for non-smokers. These tins were often sent home by the men at the front in order to be kept as a souvenir. On a local level, Northampton had a Children's Christmas Dinner Fund. Some of the money from the fund went towards the purchasing of medals and the medals. Then presented to all children aged between 3 and 14 whose fathers were away on active service. The medal was inscribed with the words, 'A recognition of my father's patriotism'.

An artist's impression, from the Northampton Independent, *of the troops receiving the results of the 'Woodbines wanted' appeal.*

The Seasons Greetings
— 1917. —
From the NORTHAMPTON ALLIED WAR FUND.

Buying gifts for the troops was one of the most popular forms of charity during the war.

As the war progressed more charitable campaigns were launched. The most popular were those that supported the troops at the front. On 29 August 1914, the *Northampton Independent* published a letter from a soldier who was fighting in France. The letter went as follows: '… prey send us a packet of "Woodbines", as the French cigarettes taste like poison to us.' The letter was then turned into the 'Woodbines wanted' appeal. By 5 September 1914 the appeal had resulted in 40,000 cigarettes being sent to the front. The cigarettes were supplied by the local tobacconist Mr W. Lee, of Bridge Street and Mayfair, who provided them at 8*s* per 1,000 with no handling fee or duty to be paid. The names of the subscribers, along with the amount that they contributed, was published at the end of each edition of the *Northampton Independent*. The sum raised for the appeal increased as time went on.

The 'Woodbines wanted' appeal was not an exception during the Great War. There were many other entreaties of a similar nature and public appeals would be set up as and when money was needed. What was very important at the time was the recognition given to each person that made a contribution. Those donating the most money towards were placed at the top of the contributors' list. Like the 'Woodbines wanted' appeal, each charitable appeal would be advertised in the local papers with the contributors names printed in each edition of the newspaper. One of the most common names to appear on the contributors list was Earl Spencer. Very often, he was also the honorary president of these sorts of appeals.

As well as these larger and better-known appeals, individuals also offered their services in support of the war effort. For instance, the Northampton Pharmacists Association, who numbered seventeen individuals, all pledged to give their services in dispensing medicines free of charge to the dependants of soldiers and sailors engaged in the forces. They also supplied the ingredients for medicines at cost price without making a profit. A Mr H. Lineham organised, entirely at his own expense, fleets of cars to be available to take convalescing men from the town's hospitals into the countryside. He also arranged for those men convalescing in hospitals in the countryside to be brought into Northampton to enjoy the various forms of entertainment on offer. These outings provided the injured men with more than just entertainment for a day and gave them something to look forward to on their long road to recovery. These are just a few examples of the many ways that individuals contributed their time, effort and money for the war effort.

A ring made by William Matthews for his wife whilst he was a prisoner of war in Germany.

Prisoner of War Funds

At the start of the war the German Government had no central authority responsible for prisoners of war. The Germans, like most other European nations, did not expect the war to last very long and, as a result, they had made no official provision for the housing of prisoners. Each German army corps was therefore responsible for the prisoners that it took in battle. The camps were run by a commandant who was entitled to run the camp as he saw fit. In consequence, the provisions within each camp

Friday, September 27th

BAND PROGRAMME

Band of H.M. 1st Life Guards

By permission Lieut.-Col. S. G. Holford, K.C.V.O., C.I.E.
Commanding 1st Regt. of Life Guards Reserve

AT 3 & 7 P.M.

Band of 2nd Batt. Northants Regt.

By permission of Major W. B. Woodham and Officers

AT 1 & 5 P.M.

MR. GEORGE MILLER, L.R.A.M.
Conductor of Band of H.M. 1st Life Guards

MR. TRAYTON ADAMS
Conductor of Band of 2nd Batt. Northants Regt.

PRICE : TWOPENCE

Many fund-raisers were held in the town to support charities, such as the Prisoner of War Funds.

varied greatly. Some camps, such as Minden and Limburg, were particularly well known for having a harsh regime.

The Prisoner of War Fund began in 1914 by supporting fifteen local men who had been captured and sent to the newly formed prisoner-of-war camps. The Red Cross, working alongside the Order of St John, formed the Central Prisoners of War Committee. This committee was responsible for raising funds for the purchasing of food, clothing and other goods that were then sent to the prisoners in Germany. The men of the Northamptonshire Regiment were also catered for by the Northamptonshire Regiment Prisoner of War Fund. By 1918 they had dispatched 70,000 parcels of food and by April of 1918 the fund had raised £26,840 through donations and charity events in and around the town. However, the committee was becoming increasingly overstretched due to the number of men from the regiment that had been taken prisoner. They had 700 men on their books, who were costing them £520 per week. In desperation the committee wrote to the council asking for assistance with the fund. The letter went as follows: 'the strain upon our fund has been so severe since the calamity to the Regiment at the Battle of the Dunes that we have paid all our outstanding accounts, we shall have only £126 in hand'. In addition to this plea, the committee also pointed out that Norfolk Council had contributed £1,100 towards the Norfolk's regimental fund. They also laboured to point out that the Northamptonshire Committee was one of only three commit- tees in Britain not to have appealed to the Central Prisoner of War Committee for funds, for which they had received a letter of thanks from the Army Council. This was all in vain as the council refused to contribute, stating that as the regiment had started to recruit nationally it could not use the taxpayers of Northampton's money until the Central Committee had been consulted.

On 1 December 1917 it was announced that the next of kin of any man who had been taken prisoner could send a parcel, not exceeding 11lb, every three months to their relative. The items that could be sent were limited to the following:

Pipe, Sponge, Pencils, Tooth Powder, Pomade, Cap Badge, Badges of Rank, Shaving Razor, Bootlaces, Pipe Lights, Handkerchief, Health Salts, Insecticide powder, Braces (not containing rubber or leather), Housewife sewing kit, Combs and Hair Brush, Clothes Brush, Games such as chess or Dominoes, Dubbin, Hobnails, Sweets, Medal Ribbon, Brass Polish, Mittens.

The parcel had to be packed by the soldiers' next of kin and not by a care committee. If any items were included that were not on the list then it could result in the whole parcel being confiscated.

By the end of the war Northampton had sent 85,985 parcels to prisoners of war. Money was raised for the fund in a variety of ways, with activities ranging from charity whist drives to concerts and fairs in Abington Park. By 1918 the British blockade on Germany had really taken its toll on German food supplies and many prisoners, via their food parcels, were better fed than the soldiers guarding them.

YMCA

The Young Man's Christian Association (YMCA) was one of the most important voluntary organisations during the First World War. The organisation provided comfort and support for servicemen both at home and overseas. On the Western Front they provided soldiers with everything from cups of tea and pocket Bibles to paper and pencils.

The YMCA also supported the troops billeted in Northampton and there were various locations where soldiers could go to rest and relax. The most grand of these was in the old Corn Exchange building, which boasted concerts, games, refreshments and, most importantly, a warm and Christian welcome to all. It was adorned in patriotic bunting and housed eight full-size billiard tables.

THANKS FOR THE PINEAPPLES
The following letter of thanks reveals just how varied the contents of gift boxes for the troops could be: 'On behalf of the NCOs and men of the 1st Northants Yeomanry, I wish to thank you most sincerely for the fifteen cases of pineapple which have arrived safely ... yours truly, T.E. Manning.'

ZEPPELIN L45

The L45, which bombed Northampton, was 650ft long and filled with hydrogen gas. It was powered by six 240hp engines, which could power the aircraft to speeds of 6mph at an altitude of approximately 20,000ft. The crew wore paper underwear and leather flying clothing to cope with freezing temperatures that could get as low as -8 degrees.

The YMCA turned the old Corn Exchange into a place of recreation for the troops. At the rear of the photo can be seen the distinctive red triangle of the YMCA.

Another location was the new Co-operative building. The Northampton Co-operative Society was growing prior to the First Word War and decided that their new central location in Abington Street would need to be expanded. As a result, they purchased the old carriage-manufacturing premises next door. Construction was under way in 1914 with the estimated completion date being 1916. A reduction in manpower and a shortage of materials prevented the premises from being finished. As construction could not be completed, the society allowed the YMCA to establish a rest room for wounded soldiers on the whole ground floor. This arrangement lasted for four years and it wasn't until 1919 that arrangements were made for the shop fittings to finally be installed on the ground floor.

The YMCA also created establishments on the Wellingborough Road, the Racecourse, Kingsthorpe, Pattishall internment/ prisoner-of-war camp and Duston War Hospital, and they even had an establishment at the train station for troops passing

through the town. The YMCA's work was all supported by voluntary subscription. As well as donating money, many people from Northampton gave their time to help run the establishments. This also included many of the musically talented members of the public who helped to provide concert parties for the troops. One of the most popular acts to perform was Miss Madge Law and her 'Merrie Makers'.

Northampton's Tank Bank

In addition to all of the local fund-raising that occurred in Northampton during the Great War, the government sought to raise funds by encouraging people to buy War Bonds and War Saving Certificates. War Bonds could be purchased in multiples of £5 and yielded 2 per cent after five years and then 5 per cent after ten years, in addition to the interest. The government promised that the security of the investment was 'the finest in the world – the guarantee of the British Empire'. The War Saving Certificates were more affordable and were therefore more accessible to a greater number of people. These could be purchased at 15s 6d and would yield £1 after five years, in addition to interest.

As well as raising money for the government's war effort, the bonds and certificates took money out of circulation, which helped to decrease inflation. The interest rate that investors received was below that of the standard market rate, however, and so patriotic messages were necessary to encourage people to invest in a scheme that yielded less than the average rate available. As part of this scheme a national Tank Bank was set up. Six Mark IV tanks toured the towns and cities of Britain in order to encourage people to invest and Northampton was one of the towns chosen to receive one such Tank Bank. Northampton's Tank Bank, opened ceremonially by the Lord Lieutenant Earl Spencer, the mayor and various other dignitaries from the town and county, was located in the Market Square from 25 February to 2 March 1918 and opened daily from 11 a.m. until 9 p.m. The government encouraged

M. S. Certificate is kept in E. A.'s box at Bank.

Northamptonshire Union Bank Limited.

Received of Mr E. A. Law

Thirty one pounds on Account of

War Savings Certificate — 2 Mar 1918

For the Directors & Proprietors.

£ 31.—

BRITISH TANKS
2 MR
18
W.S.A.

War Saving Certificates were sold by local banks. These certificates helped to reduce inflation by taking money out of circulation.

a competitive spirit between the various towns that the tanks visited; the town that invested the most money per capita would win a tank. Unfortunately, Northampton came third but it did invest a considerable amount of money. By the end of the war Northampton had contributed over £8 million to the various War Bonds and War Saving schemes.

Inflation, Food Prices and Rationing

Apart from the panic buying of food in the early weeks of the conflict, the majority of the war years didn't see a chronic shortage of food in Britain. For working-class people the problem was not so much the availability of food but the cost of it. Before 1914 yearly inflation was in the region of around 1 to 2 per cent, during the course of the war this rose to around 25 to 30 per cent, and by 1918 retail prices had more than doubled. Bread that sold for 4*d* a loaf in 1914 had increased in price to 11½*d* by the end of 1917. The situation was exacerbated in 1917 when the German Navy launched its campaign of unrestricted submarine warfare. This new German policy was especially hard-hitting for the British people since a large proportion of the nation's food was imported and the wheat harvest in the winter of 1916 had been particularly poor.

INSURE
SUCCESS IN TRENCHES BY SAVING AT TABLE.

FOOD IS VICTORY.

Every ounce of food saved adds to the country's fighting strength. Prussia wants to take away our bread, hence her U-boats. Food Saving will defeat the enemy's plans.

JOIN
LEAGUE OF  THE
NATIONAL SAFETY.

Applications to be   addressed to the
MINISTRY OF FOOD,   Grosvenor House, London,
W.1.

NOTE THESE FACTS.

1. Food Savers are Ship Savers.

2. America and Canada are eating less to ensure victory. We mustn't waste what they save. America needs ships to send soldiers to Europe. Food saved means soldiers in France.

3. Food is precious as gold. What's money worth if there's no food ?

4. "I can't save much." But everybody's little makes the great whole. Begin to-day.

5. Your rations, state-fixed or free, still allow food-saving and sacrifice for country.

FOOD SAVERS ARE SHIP SAVERS.

(B 10972) Wt.   —g 391 1500M 11/17 H & S

'Success in the trenches by saving at table.' Although not as refined as the propaganda of the Second World War, this rationing leaflet clearly gets the message across.

Ration books were introduced to ensure that everyone got their fair share of produce. Even soldiers on leave had to have their own ration books.

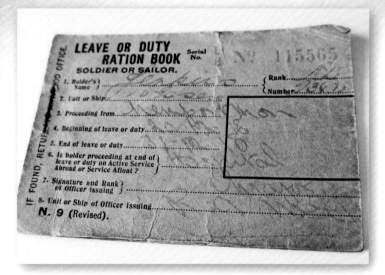

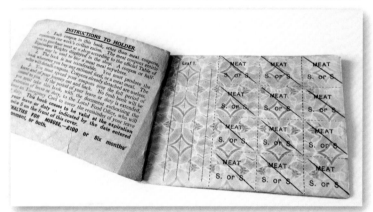

At this point the British Government realised that the nation's food supplies were becoming vulnerable and tried to curtail the populations' food consumption by introducing a policy of voluntary rationing. The royal family added their support to the scheme and propaganda posters and leaflets tried to encourage the population to reduce its food consumption in order to ensure victory in the trenches. The government was especially keen to limit the public's consumption of bread, as Britain was heavily reliant upon the importation of wheat. Unfortunately, the government's propaganda campaign failed. As a result, mandatory rationing was introduced in early 1918. Sugar was one of the first things to be rationed followed by meat, butter, cheese and margarine. Not surprisingly the introduction of rationing was not very popular in war-weary Northampton. Along with the introduction of

Frugality became the order of the day during the war. Prices steadily rose and eventually rationing was introduced.

rationing, a new national phenomenon was sweeping the country: the queue. The limited food supply, plus the addition of rationing paperwork and the limited number of shop assistants all helped to create this new social ritual.

Although the cost of food rose throughout the war it must be remembered that wages also increased as well. For those who worked in high-paid industries, such as the munitions industry, wages were high. In fact, wages kept to around 10 to 20 per cent ahead of the cost of living. There were two problems, however. Wage rises did not always occur in conjunction with price rises and secondly those people who no longer worked or who had a large number of dependents were worse off than before the war.

How to Reduce your Bread Bill

PURITY

A timely suggestion by
W. Q. ADAMS
TO THE CAREFUL HOUSEWIFE

THE SILENT RAID

During the Great War nearly 9,000 German bombs were dropped on Great Britain over the course of 103 air raids. Northampton experienced one of these raids on the night of 19 October 1917 when Zeppelin L45, commanded by Kapitanleutnant Kolle, bombed the town. The L45 was one of thirteen airships that were destined to raid Britain that night in what was to become the largest raid of the war. The attack, which was part of a larger German operation, became known as the Silent Raid because the aircraft were flying at altitudes of up to 20,000ft and could not be heard from the ground. Fear of confrontation with British fighters had driven the Germans up to such high altitudes.

The L45 took off from Tondern armed with 2x300kg and 14x50kg high-explosive bombs and ten incendiary bombs, with the intention of bombing Sheffield. While crossing the English Channel the L45 was attacked by British aircraft and, in order to elude the attackers, the Zeppelin gained in altitude only to be blown south by extreme winds. By 10.45 p.m. the L45 crossed over Northampton. The Zeppelin's logbook tells us that the crew were unaware of what town they were over but, seeing an opportune target, they decided to drop nine incendiary bombs. The intelligence report, compiled after the raid using the captured logbook and interviews with the crew, states: 'The first instalments of bombs were dropped and the crew imagined that they must have damaged some factories in the neighbourhood of Oxford.' One of the bombs fell on No. 46 Parkwood Street, St James End. Asleep upstairs was Mrs Eliza Gammons and her twin daughters, Gladys and Lily, aged just 13 years old. Mrs Gammons was killed instantly when the incendiary bomb crashed through the roof and into her bedroom. Private Albert Bazeley of the Army Veterinary Corps, who was Mrs Gammon's son-in-law, was able to get upstairs, fight through the flames and rescue the twins by lowering them out of their bedroom before making his own escape. He subsequently helped to break the front door down and fight the fire. Despite this most heroic act, the twins died shortly afterwards due to the burns they had sustained.

Zeppelin L45 then made its way on to London where it dropped bombs on Piccadilly Circus before turning back across the English Channel. Unfortunately for the crew of L45, it was unable to make its way to either Germany or neutral Switzerland and, due to loss of engine power, it landed near Sisteron in southern France. The crew set fire to the Zeppelin and then surrendered. In all, their mission had lasted some twenty hours and much of that time had been spent in sub-zero temperatures. Karl Schuz, the executive officer of L45, had previously taken part in six raids over England and the Silent Raid would prove to be his last. When interviewed in 1964 about his experience during the Silent Raid, one of Schuz's overriding memories was of one of his engineers being intoxicated by leaking gas. This intoxication, combined with the effects of altitude sickness, caused the engineer to become disorientated, stumble and fall 18,000ft to his death. Of a total of thirteen Zeppelins that took part in the Silent Raid four of the Zeppelins were destroyed.

Background image – The grave of Eliza,
Gladys and Lily Gammons in Dallington Cemetery.

All Pulling Together?

As much as we would all like to think that the town pulled together during the Great War, this was not always the case. What often started as small and petty issues often escalated into larger ones where people's patriotism was put into question. For instance, several Volunteer Aid Detachment (VAD) nurses travelling on a tram in December 1914 were 'rudely' asked in front of other

Picture postcards were an important part of communicating during the war.

passengers to pay full fare for their journey, when the fare, like travel for troops, should have been half price. The incident was reported in the papers with great fervour and then taken up with the town council. It was agreed by the Tramways Committee to issue free passes thereafter for VAD nurses who were going about their duty.

Other newspaper reports contain letters from residents complaining about the number of drunken soldiers in the Wellingborough Road area. Questions were raised about their contribution to the war effort and, more to the point, why the publicans were allowed to profiteer from such activities. The likelihood is that the number of these incidents was actually very small, especially when it is considered that at some points there were up to 16,000 soldiers billeted in and around the town.

LOVE WILL LIVE LONGER THAN ROSES (1).
I still have the rose that you gave me, long, long ago it seems,
I hold it to-night in the dim twilight, as your face in the firelight gleams ;
Only a rose fast fading, tender'd at parting, dear,
But I gaze in its heart as the grey shadows start, and these words I seem to hear.

War-themed designs were produced both in Britain and in France in order to ensure that relatives could keep in touch.

After the deadly Zeppelin raid on Northampton in October 1917, the *Northampton Independent*'s Jupiter was, as usual, unequivocally forthright in his views on those of the town who were not doing their bit: 'I have formed the conclusion that lights are used in the back part of houses not open to observation from the street [away from the prying eyes of Special Constables] in a perfectly reckless manner … these thoughtless people imperil the lives and property of all of us.'

In addition to these petty local squabbles, some Northampton citizens voiced their opinion that Great Britain should not be at war at all. In August 1914, the Religious Society of Friends set these principles down in print, publishing a leaflet entitled 'To Men and Women of Good Will in the British Empire'. The leaflet

SOCIAL ACTIVITIES
During good weather, popular concerts were held in Abington Park. Famous regimental bands, such as the Grenadier and Coldstream Guards, would play for the assembled crowd. The Northampton Training Corps also formed a band, which on occasion played at the Abington concerts.

insisted that the war was 'unchristian', a 'gigantic folly' and that 'the war should be brought to an end at the earliest possible moment'. During August 1916 a series of public anti-war meetings were held in the Market Square. Harold Croft spoke at one of these meetings and praised the good work being done by those opposing the conscription of workers into the forces. He even admitted to being a conscientious objector during one of his speeches.

The following extract from the *Northampton Independent* on 28 December 1918 shows that there were often tensions between those who went to fight and those who stayed at home:

Personally, I know of numerous cases of men getting into munitions factories to dodge military service and earning more money than they ever hoped to see. I have neighbours who escaped the army this way, and who have positively rioted in their new found prosperity. They have spent lavishly, saving nothing for a rainy day, and now expect the public, among whom are ex-soldiers, disabled while protecting them, to be taxed to maintain them. Signed Tommy.

6

COMING HOME

It is consciousness of the awful price we have paid for victory that has caused the rejoicing among soldiers to be more subdued than the rejoicing among civilians. Armageddon has come and gone, but its consequences will continue for generations.

Northampton Independent, *16 November 1918*.

The Good News

The good news was reported in the *Northampton Daily Echo* on 11 November 1918:

The glad news we print today fills all hearts with joy. After four-and-a-quarter years of terrible conflict, the war is ended … and our hearts go out in glad greeting to the men who on the battlefronts and on the seas and in the air, this morning received the signal that they had done their work and earned the guerdon of rest. With what joy shall we welcome them home and those who never will return – we do not forget them even in these hours of proud elation. There is sorrow as well as joy in our hearts and a tender sympathy for every home in which the happiness of today is chilled by the remembrance of dear ones who have died for the cause.

News of the Armistice spread around the town like wildfire. Windows were flung open, factories and schools shut, church bells rang, spontaneous dancing ensured and cries of 'it's over' echoed throughout the streets. As if from nowhere, flags and bunting were strung from buildings. In many of the factories there was spontaneous rejoicing and cheers and singing of patriotic songs quickly drowned out the noise of machinery. One factory owner gave his recollection of the events in his factory to the *Northampton Daily Echo*: 'Our factory was like a concert hall when the news reached us. We simply could not hold our people. They were so delighted that they felt they could not work and put on their coats and hats and left the factory for the day.' Crowds of children and soldiers started to fill the once-quiet streets and there was even an impromptu procession of children dressed as German prisoners

The jubilant scene of victory. This photograph was taken looking south down the Drapery.

The nurses of Northampton Hospital parade at the end of the war.

of war, guarded by a khaki-clad guard. The volunteer band, supported by the voices of the massed crowd, played patriotic songs in the Market Square. All recruiting of men for the army was stopped immediately and call-up papers were cancelled.

The next morning the town settled back down to ordinary life. People went back to their normal routines and, apart from a few leftover pieces of bunting and some flags, there were no outward signs to differentiate peace from war. For many people the momentary celebrations were marred by the knowledge of the final cost of the nation's victory. It was noted at the time that the majority of those waving flags and singing songs were the young. The older generations were far more contemplative. They knew that life had changed forever. Even those who had men coming back home knew that the future would be uncertain.

On the Western Front, on the day of the Armistice, the men of the 1st Battalion Northamptonshire Regiment were addressed by Lieutenant Colonel G.St.G. Robinson, DSO, MC:

> … I often think it is one of the most frightening things to belong to a fine regiment like this and to know what a high standard we must sustain, but, by God you men of the 48th have kept it well. Most of you come from Northamptonshire, and I say with certainty no county should be prouder of her men.

The Boys are Back

Although the signing of the Armistice brought the war to an end it did not mean that men could return to their families straight away. Ron James, who served with the 48th Regiment, later recalled: 'Now that the war was at an end we thought our next move would be home and demobilisation, but the army thought otherwise and our long march started to the Rhine. We followed on the heels of the German Army, who were making their way back to their own country.' The surrender and occupation of Germany had first to be arranged and the battlefields, destroyed villages and towns of France and Flanders had to be cleared of the detritus of war. Much of this work was not only difficult but also dangerous, due to the amount of unexploded ordnance. Equipment needed to be cleaned, counted and returned to depots, and the many horses that the army took to France needed to be either returned to England or sold on. There were still lots to do before the men could return home.

There was no mass return of men and each battalion of the Northamptonshire Regiment came back individually. On their return, each battalion was welcomed home both informally

Northampton Daily Echo, 28 April 1919, reporting upon the return of the 2nd Battalion Northamptonshire Regiment:

'A wonderful reception, participated in by everyone from the Lord Lieutenant of the county to the smallest street urchin, was accorded the cadre of the 2nd Battalion Northamptonshire Regiment on Saturday Evening.'

by the town's people and officially by representatives of the council and the town's great and good.

The 2nd Battalion Northamptonshire Regiment was the first battalion to return from the Western Front. It was also the first chance that the townspeople had had to officially welcome home their victorious men and well-wishers turned out in their hundreds to cheer the soldiers home. The return journey had been a long and difficult one and local newspapers followed the slow and rough progress of the 2nd Battalion as they travelled through France, over the Channel and finally back to Britain. On 28 April 1919 the *Northampton Chronicle* was finally able to paint this vivid picture of the men's homecoming:

There had been some cheering as the men came from the station, but their exit from its precincts was the signal for a tremendous outburst. From this moment until the last man had entered the Guildhall the streets echoed and re-echoed with the volleys of hurrahs, in which the crowd found relief for their pent-up war feelings.

Presentation of medals to a sergeant in the Northamptons.

Medals awarded to Sergeant W.E. Boulter VC.

An official reception, along with medal presentations and speeches, was put on for the men at the Guildhall. This official reception was to make up for the fact that the Northamptonshire Yeomanry had returned two weeks early but the council had not been given enough notice by the military authority in order to prepare an official celebration. The yeoman had an unofficial welcome as they paraded from the train station through the town on their way back to the Drill Hall. Upon reaching the Drill Hall, the local men were dismissed to their homes, whilst non-local men were put up in nearby billets.

The 7th Battalion Northamptonshire Regiment, on the other hand, did not all return at the same time. Following the Armistice the battalion had spent seven months abroad prior to their demobilisation. In 1919 the first party of six other ranks was dispatched for Northampton and, thereafter, men were sent back in a piecemeal fashion, in small groups one to two times per week. Eventually all

EKFORD'S KIOSK
Frank Ekford lost a leg in the First World War. Inspired by his time in Paris, Ekford decided that he wanted to open his own news and cigarettes kiosk. Supported by the British Legion, and with the help of the council, he was able to establish a kiosk outside of All Saints church. Although he died in 1924, the kiosk continued and remained a much-loved landmark in the town centre until the 1970s.

Although victorious, the town did not forget at what price victory was paid for. Numerous services were held around Northampton to remember those who gave their lives and to give thanks for those who returned.

National Union of Railwaymen

NORTHAMPTON BRANCH

Memorial Service

For Members who died in the Great War, 1914-1918, held in The Church of St. Mary, Far Cotton, Northampton, on Sunday, 5th of October, 1919, at Three o'clock.

MEMBERS ARE AT LIBERTY to KEEP this ORDER OF SERVICE AS A MEMENTO OF THE OCCASION

that was left of the battalion was a small cadre of five officers and fifty-one other ranks who volunteered to stay behind and ensure that the battalion's equipment was taken charge of and was properly accounted for until it could be handed back to the various quarter-masters. On 14 June 1919 the cadre was welcomed home at the station by the mayor, a guard of honour and ex-members of the battalion. They marched through the town amidst jubilant scenes as they made their way to the Town Hall, where they were treated to a luncheon and speeches of welcome and thanks were given. Soon after this the battalion was disbanded and the 7th Battalion Northamptonshire Regiment was no more. The 6th Battalion Northamptonshire Regiment was, unfortunately, disbanded in France and therefore the town was deprived of the chance to give them a proper welcome home.

As part of his demobilisation, Charles Crutchley was given a medical examination in Le Havre. After his medical he was treated to a hot shower and it so happened that the shower's attendant was a German prisoner of war. The two men struck up a conversation. The German discussed his wife and family back in Germany and his job as a schoolteacher. Both men agreed that the war had been the war to end all wars and it must never happen again. The German concluded that 'we, the ordinary people, suffer more than any because of war'. Ron James also had a similar experience whilst billeted with a German family:

Memorial service missalette.

Long years ago, as earth lay dark and still,
Rose a loud cry upon a lonely hill,
While in the frailty of our human clay
Christ, our Redeemer, passed the self-same way.

Still stands His Cross from that dread hour to this
Like some bright star above the dark abyss;
Still, through the veil, the Victor's pitying eyes
Look down to bless our lesser Calvaries.

These were his servants, in his steps they trod,
Following through death the martyr'd Son of God;
Victor He rose; victorious too shall rise
They who have drunk His cup of sacrifice.

O risen Lord, O Shepherd of our dead,
Whose Cross has bought them and Whose Staff has led,
In glorious hope their proud and sorrowing land
Commits her children to Thy gracious hand.   Amen.

Sermon.

Hymn

(During which a collection will be made for the Blind)

SON of God, eternal Saviour,
    Source of life and truth, and grace,
Son of man, Whose birth incarnate
    Hallows all our human race,
Thou, our Head, Who, throned in glory,
    For Thine own dost ever plead,
Fill us with Thy love and pity,
    Heal our wrongs and help our need.

As Thou, Lord, hast lived for others,
    So may we for others live;
Freely have Thy gifts been granted,
    Freely may Thy servants give.
Thine the gold and Thine the silver,
    Thine the wealth of land and sea,
We but stewards of Thy bounty,
    Held in solemn trust for Thee.

Come, O Christ, and reign among us,
    King of Love, and Prince of Peace,
Hush the storm of strife and passion,
    Bid its cruel discords cease:
By Thy patient years of toiling,
    By Thy silent hours of pain,
Quench our fevered thirst of pleasure,
    Shame our selfish greed of gain.

Ah, the past is dark behind us,
    Strewn with wrecks and stained with blood;
But before us gleams the vision
    Of the coming brotherhood.
See the Christlike host advancing,
    High and lowly, great and small,
Linked in bonds of common service
    For the common Lord of all.

Son of God, eternal Saviour,
    Source of life and truth and grace,
Son of man Whose birth incarnate
    Hallows all our human race,
Thou Who prayedst, Thou Who willest
    That Thy people should be one,
Grant, O grant our hope's fruition:
    Here on earth Thy will be done.   Amen.

The Blessing.

… our hosts were almost at starvation point, so we helped them out when we could by supplying them with some of our own rations … through this help many friendships were formed. We also met some of the Germans who had fought against us and discussed past times with them. There was no animosity, for we were all fellow sufferers of the same conflict.

Memorial service missalette continued.

Order of Service

Hymn.

O GOD our help in ages past,
Our hope for years to come,
Our shelter from the stormy blast,
And our eternal home.

Beneath the shadow of Thy throne
Thy saints have dwelt secure;
Sufficient is Thine arm alone,
And our defence is sure.

Before the hills in order stood,
Or earth received her frame,
From everlasting Thou art God,
To endless years the same.

A thousand ages in Thy sight
Are like an evening gone;
Short as the watch that ends the night
Before the rising sun.

Time, like an ever rolling stream,
Bears all its sons away;
They fly forgotten, as a dream
Dies at the opening day.

O God, our help in ages past,
Our hope for years to come,
Be Thou our guard while troubles last,
And our eternal home. Amen.

The Roll of Honour will here be read.

GREATER love hath no man than this, that a man lay down his life for his friends.

Then shall be sung :

I AM the Resurrection and the Life, saith the Lord; he that believeth in me, though he were dead, yet shall he live; and whosoever liveth and believeth in Me shall never die.

I HEARD a voice from heaven saying unto me, Write, From henceforth blessed are the dead which die in the Lord; even so saith the Spirit; for they rest from their labours.

Lesson.

Hymn.

THINK, O Lord, in mercy
On the souls of those
Who, in faith gone from us,
Now in death repose.

Here, 'mid stress and conflict,
Toils can never cease;
There, the warfare ended,
Bid them rest in peace.

Often were they wounded
In the deadly strife,
Heal them, Good Physician,
With the balm of life.

Every taint of evil,
Frailty and decay,
Good and gracious Saviour,
Cleanse and purge away.

Rest eternal grant them,
After weary fight;
Shed on them the radiance
Of Thy heavenly light.

Lead them onward, upward,
To the holy place
Where Thy saints, made perfect,
Gaze upon Thy face. Amen.

Let us pray.

OUR Father, ... deliver us from evil. Amen.

A Thanksgiving for the good example of those who have died.

O God of the spirits of all flesh, we praise and magnify Thy holy Name for all Thy servants who, having fought a good fight, have finished their course in Thy faith and fear; and we beseech Thee that, encouraged by their examples and strengthened by their fellowship, we with them may be found meet to be partakers of the inheritance of the saints in light; through the merits of Thy son, Jesus Christ our Lord. Amen.

A Commendation of the fallen.

ALMIGHTY God, we commend to Thy loving kindness the souls of Thy servants, our brothers, who have given their lives to defend us. Accept, O Lord, the offering of their self-sacrifice, and grant to them with all Thy faithful servants a place of refreshment and peace, where the light of Thy countenance shines for ever, and where all tears are wiped away; through Jesus Christ our Lord. Amen.

A Prayer for all who suffer.

UNTO Thy loving kindness, O Lord, we commend all those who are stricken and suffering by reason of the war: the wounded, the disabled, and the blind; all who have been bereaved of those dear to them; all whose faith in Thee has been shaken by what they have seen or suffered. Strengthen them, O Lord, with Thy Holy Spirit, and give them courage and hope. Help us to do our part in ministering to them; for the sake of Him Who bore for us the pain and desolation of the Cross, Thy Son our Saviour Jesus Christ. Amen.

A Dedication of ourselves to righteousness.

O LORD Christ Thou Prince of Peace, the faithful and true, who in righteousness dost judge and make war; grant to us all, we beseech Thee, that, putting on the whole armour of God, we may follow Thee as Thou goest forth conquering and to conquer; and, fighting manfully under Thy banner against sin, the world, and the devil, we may be found more than conquerors, and at the last may be refreshed with the multitude of peace in the holy City of our God; Whose is the greatness and the power, the victory and the majesty for evermore. Amen.

A Prayer of fellowship and service.

OPEN our eyes, O Lord, at this time to know Thy will: guide and strengthen us to fulfil it. Delivered by Thy mercy from the perils of war, and united in true fellowship with one another, may we find in Thy service our perfect freedom; through Jesus Christ our Lord. Amen.

Hymn

O VALIANT hearts who to your glory came
Through dust of conflict and through battle flame;
Tranquil you lie, your knightly virtue proved,
Your memory hallowed in the land you loved.

Proudly you gathered, rank on rank, to war,
As who had heard God's message from afar;
All you had hoped for, all you had, you gave
To save mankind— yourselves you scorned to save.

Splendid you passed, the great surrender made,
Into the light that never more shall fade;
Deep your contentment in that blessed abode,
Who wait the last clear trumpet-call of God.

TRENCH ART
AND MEMENTOS

Many of the soldiers returning from active service with the army bought back mementos of their time abroad. Some of these items are commonly described as trench art and were decorative items made out of old shell cases and other redundant pieces of military hardware. The term is somewhat of a misnomer, however, as most of the pieces were not actually produced in the trenches themselves but behind the line during rest periods. The embossing of metal, using a hammer and chisel, would have been too loud an activity to carry out in the trenches and such activity would only have brought unwanted attention from the enemy in the form of an artillery bombardment. A lot of the pieces were produced by local French civilians and sold to the soldiers in shops and cafes. As well as making decorative souvenirs out of old shell cases, soldiers would often carve the soft chalk that was found in areas such as Loos. Unlike a lot of trench art, this almost silent activity was safe to carry out in front-line trenches. Regimental cap badges were one of the most popular images to carve.

Other popular mementos included embroidered silks, which were often produced by local women and sold to soldiers whilst they were at rest behind the lines, and photographic postcards. For a fee travelling photographers would take a photograph, develop it, and then post it to the specified address in Britain.

A small handmade regimental cushion.

Heroes Day

Heroes Day was held on 6 September 1919 as an official celebration giving thanks to all of Northampton's sons who had served their nation in a time of great need. Having welcomed the battalions home one by one, Heroes Day was a way for the town to celebrate all of their achievements with the maximum amount of fanfare.

The day started with 8,000 ex-servicemen marching eight abreast through the town centre, passing the temporary cenotaph that had been erected outside the new Co-operative building on Abington Street, and on into Abington Park. In the park, a series of marquees had been erected and a victory meal was served. The meal was so large that it accounted for nine bullocks, six sheep, 350 hams, 1,000lb of corned beef, 20,000 rolls, 24,000 pastries and 43,300 half pints of beer. In total, it amounted to 100 tons of transported goods! The provision of such large quantities of food was no easy task and it would not have been possible without an army of volunteer helpers.

Soon after Heroes Day, on 24 October 1919, the town was gifted with a tank. The plan was to drive it up to Abington Park where a ceremony would be held and the tank would be unveiled and officially named Steelbacks. The ceremony had to be cancelled, however, as the 28-ton tank broke down at several different intervals along the way and was unable to get to the park on time. When the tank eventually made it to Abington Park it was put on display and served as an unofficial climbing frame for the town's

The temporary cenotaph that was placed outside the Co-operative building for Heroes Day in 1919.

THEIR NAME SHALL LIVE FOR EVERMORE

OUR GLORIOUS DEAD

NORTHAMPTON · 1919.

youngsters. After some years of neglect, the town council voted to remove it in 1934. The view of many people in the town was that it was not only becoming an eyesore but was an unnecessary object that glorified war. As a result, the tank was cut into pieces and sent to a scrapyard in 1935.

Rewards and Recognition of Service

There were five campaign medals available for those who saw service in the First World War, and individuals would automatically receive two or three medals, depending upon when and where they had served. These medals were issued by the government but the high demand meant that there was often a lengthy delay before men received them and many soliders did not obtain theirs until the 1920s. Each medal was individually engraved with the recipient's service number, rank, name and unit.

The British War Medal and the Victory Medal were the most common campaign medals. The British War Medal was awarded to anyone who had rendered 'approved' service. The Victory Medal, as the name suggests, was awarded to mark the end of hostilities and was awarded to anyone who had entered a theatre of war. It was of a standard design that was shared by all of the Allied nations.

Individuals who saw service before 1 January 1916 qualified for one of two other campaign medals. Those who saw service between 4 August 1914 and 22 November 1914 were entitled to the 1914 Star. This is sometimes known as the Mons Star as it was commonly awarded to the 'Old Contemptibles' who were the first men of the British Expeditionary Force to see service at the start of the war. The 1914–15 Star was issued to those who saw service between 22 November 1914 and 31 December 1915.

DEMOBILISATION

When the war was over, men wanted to get back to their families as quickly as possible. It was not, however, a fast or simple process. With so many men to get through and with a formal system of demobilisation to follow, men were demobilised in batches. Those who worked in vital industries were first, followed by the early war volunteers. This left those men who had been conscripted in the later years of the war until last.

The Victory Medal.

When the 1914 Star or the 1914–15 Star is worn alongside the British War Medal and the Victory Medal they are unofficially know as 'Pip, Squeak and Wilfred'. This nickname is attributable to a popular comic strip of the same name that was prevalent in the 1920s. How and why the nickname came about is not known.

The Territorial Force War Medal was the least commonly awarded campaign medal. It was only awarded to those of the Territorial Force who had served for four years prior to the start of the war and who were not entitled to either the 1914 Star or the 1914–15 Star. Only 33,944 of these medals were awarded compared to the 6,610,000 British War Medals.

Memorial Plaques, often known as Death Plaques or Death Pennies, were issued by the government to the next of kin of anyone who died from any cause – enemy fire, accident or illness at home or abroad – during the war. The plaques were made from bronze and were individually marked with the individual's name.

No rank is shown on the plaque and the design is the same for officers and enlisted men to show that in death all men are equal. The plaque came in a protective cardboard box along with an illuminated scroll.

Sadly, some people were so impoverished during the interwar years that they were forced to sell the plaques for scrap metal. Being constructed of bronze they were of good value and were bought by pawnbrokers.

The King's Roll

The King's Roll was established in 1919 under the National Scheme for the Employment of Disabled Ex-Servicemen. The aim of the nationwide scheme was to provide employment for all disabled ex-servicemen and to have every company employing as many ex-servicemen as they could.

RE-ENLISTING
In order to keep an army of occupation in Germany, the army encouraged men who had enlisted 'for the duration of the war' to re-enlist in 1919. Many men did re-enlist and took the sizeable bounty that came with it. Those who signed on for twenty-seven months would receive a £20 bounty whilst those signing on for fifty-one months received a substantial bounty of £50.

In order to qualify for the scheme an employer had to have no fewer than 5 per cent of their entire workforce comprising of disabled ex-servicemen.

All employers who enrolled in the scheme had their company's names added to the King's Roll at a national and local level. Like many other schemes and fund-raisers that ran during the war, the social importance of these rolls was very significant as signing up to the scheme was a way of showing that you were an upstanding member of the community. By 1920 fifty-eight companies had signed up but it was reported in the *Northampton Independent* that 200 'large employers' had still yet to do so. On 14 September 1920, the mayor wrote an open letter to local businessmen: 'In other districts it has been found possible, as a result of good-will from all concerned, to absorb all the disabled men into employment, and I am most anxious that we should achieve the same success here.' It took the Borough Council until 1923 to sign up to the scheme. After a slow start, the council continued with the scheme all the way up until 1941 when the council had to stop due to the demands of the Second World War.

The Ex-Servicemen's Club

Today, ex-servicemen's clubs are a common sight in many towns and cities across the country. Except for a few such clubs in London, these institutions did not really exist before the Great War. In Northampton the creation of the ex-servicemen's club was down to two gentlemen by the names of Mr A.E. Catt and Mr F.C. Parker. These two gentlemen could see the obvious advantages of creating a club for those who had returned from the front and the idea was to establish premises where ex-members of the armed forces could socialise and share their experiences. These clubs enabled men to talk to others who understood not only what they went through during the war but the various problems that they were experiencing as they readjusted to ordinary civilian life.

A public collection was carried out and a lump sum was provided from the balance of the Soldier's Comforts and

Prisoners of War funds. The £4,500 raised went to the purchasing of Kerr House, which was leased to the ex-servicemen for a mere 1s a year.

Women at Peace

When the war was over and the men started to return home, the Restoration of Pre-War Practices Act forced women to step aside and allow men back into their old jobs. This Act, combined with the decline in production and the need to care for wounded male relatives, meant that many women returned to their pre-wartime roles. Of the men who went off to fight, nine out of ten returned home and, out of that number, over 1.6 million were wounded. Some of these wounds were minor and the men made quick recoveries, but others had to live with their injuries for the rest of their lives and needed caring for by their families.

The increased birth rate in England would also have affected the need for women to return to their pre-wartime roles and to the care of the household and children. The birth rate per 1,000 people increased as follows:

1913: 24.1
1916: 20.9
1918: 17.7
1920: 25.5

There was, however, some progress in women's rights due to the war. For instance, the Sex Disqualification Act made it illegal to exclude women from jobs because of their gender and the Representation of the People Act enfranchised 8.5 million women who were over 30 years old.

A WIDOW'S PENSION
Widows pensions were graded in accordance to their late husband's rank. The 1915 regulations stated that widows of private soldiers should receive 13s 9d per week. This rose progressively through each rank, with a widow of a WO1 (rank of a sergeant major) receiving 21s and 3d per week.

A total war requires the maximisation of production on the home front. Women going into agriculture freed men up to fight as well as ensuring that enough food was produced.

Every woman who helps in agriculture during the war is as truly serving her country as the man who is fighting in the trenches or on the sea.

Walter Runciman
President of the Board of Trade

Selborne
President of the Board of Agriculture.

Impact on the Population

It is hard to find accurate figures for the number of men killed in the Great War. By comparing the 1911 and the 1921 censuses we can, however, see some overarching trends for the whole of society. For instance, the average size of a family in Northampton in the 1911 census was 4.24 – by the 1921 census this number had declined to 3.95. The number of widows in 1911 was 2,334 – this figure increased to 14,740 in 1921. Even more telling is the number of widows aged between 30 and 39 in the 1921 census:

20 to 29:	332
30 to 39:	820
40 to 59:	409
60 and over:	773

The notification of the death of a loved one was done via post during the war. No official information regarding the circumstances of death was provided.

The 1921 census shows us that the county had a population of 349,363; comprised of 168,517 males and 180,846 females. The population in 1911 was 348,515, which shows an increase in population of 848. That small increase in population, over

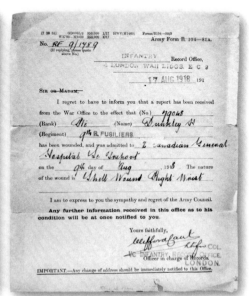

a ten-year period, can be put into perspective by comparing it with the increase from 1901 to 1911 where the population of the county rose by 12,887. The birth rate did fall during the war years due to the men being away and we also know that 6,040 men from the Northamptonshire Regiment lost their lives. Some 1,700 of these men were from Northampton but it must be noted that many of the men would not have been from the county but may have joined from elsewhere.

Influenza

The influenza epidemic of 1918, which became known as the Spanish Flu, was the worst case of its kind in history. It spread around the world and killed between 50 and 100 million people, far more than the First World War itself. Unlike other influenza outbreaks, which normally take their toll on the young, the elderly or the otherwise unhealthy, this strain of influenza attacked all and reaped a massive toll throughout the world. In Northampton, it was said that every family was affected and in some cases whole families perished. The police force was so badly hit that it required Special Constables to bolster its depleted numbers; many tram routes were cancelled due to the high toll of sickness within the Corporation's staff; and a great number of those who had survived the horrors of the trenches had their lives taken by the virus that had initially started in a British training base on the French coast before becoming an international epidemic. The Spanish Flu was perhaps one of the first signs that the future would not be as rosy as the government promised. Post-war Britain was not going to be a 'land fit for heroes'.

POSTSCRIPT

LEGACY

They gave of their best, whether it was in the mud of Flanders, the heat of the desert, or the storms of the sea or the air, and they carried on to the bitter end.

Major General John Brown addressing the crowd at the opening of the Garden of Remembrance in Abington Square, 1938

Honouring the Fallen

The Great War had a massive impact on everyday life in both Northampton and Great Britain as a whole. The people of Britain had to endure many new challenges, such as rationing, conscription and, for the first time in history, enemy attacks from the air. As a result of these challenges and many more besides, Great Britain began to change as a society. Values and attitudes started to change and this included attitudes towards the war dead. In previous conflicts, enlisted men who had died in combat would be buried together in an unmarked communal grave while officers received special treatment. During the First World War, however, men of all ranks were treated equally in death. Britain no longer had a small professional army; instead it had a civilian army, manned by people from every walk of life, every occupation and every social class. This changed the way that the general public perceived soldiers and the army.

In combat, soldiers would bury their fallen comrades in makeshift cemeteries, marking their burial plots with a wooden cross that displayed the fallen man's name. There was no official policy on the burial of soldiers and no units were created to oversee the process of recording grave locations. In 1914 the Commonwealth War Graves Commission, which now administers and oversees 940 First World War cemeteries in France and Belgium, did not yet exist. Sir Fabian Ware, a journalist and civil servant who volunteered to serve with the Red Cross in France during the war, noticed the sporadic way that many soldiers were being laid to rest and set out to ensure that all known grave locations were recorded and that all grave sites were cared for. By 1915 the army had given his team official recognition by creating the Graves Registration Commission. By May 1917 the Imperial War Graves Commission had been set up by Royal Charter.

It is due to Ware and his team that the men of Northampton, who were buried in a corner of a foreign field, are now looked after with eternal love and care in Commonwealth War Graves Commission cemeteries. At the time, however, the establishment of permanent cemeteries abroad was a very controversial issue. Many people believed that the government should have reinterred the bodies in Britain. The government, on the other hand, felt that the process would be too long, too expensive and, with so many unknown graves, too difficult. The decision was taken to leave the fallen *in situ* with their comrades, where they had lived, fought and died together.

The number of people wealthy enough to travel abroad and find the graves of their loved ones was limited, especially in the economically tough post-war years. This left a hole in many people's hearts, as they had nowhere to go in order to grieve, to remember and to pay homage. This vital part of the grieving process led to the establishment of cenotaphs around the country. Cenotaphs (simply meaning empty tomb) soon became the focal point for a town's grief and acts of remembrance. The first cenotaph was erected in Whitehall, London, in 1919. The idea soon spread across the country. Northampton's first cenotaph was in Abington Street in front of the old Co-operative building. It was made of wood and plaster and was the focal point for the Heroes Day parade.

War Graves

Northamptonshire has 704 war graves. These are spread out in 144 cemeteries and churchyards across the county. Unlike the many massed Commonwealth War Graves Commission cemeteries overseas, the war graves found in Britain are not

A Commonwealth War Graves Commission headstone at Dallington Cemetery. Headstones like this can be found in churchyards and cemeteries all around the county. Each headstone displays the name, rank, number, regiment and date of death of the solider. For a small fee families could also have a personalised message engraved at the bottom of the stone.

gathered together. As a result, many such graves can be found dotted around local cemeteries and churchyards. The varied locations of these burials is due to the dispersed nature of the many temporary hospitals that sprang up in order to cope with the casualties. The deceased would be buried locally if no other arrangements could be made.

The 704 war graves are made up of the following nationalities and arms of service:

588 British Army
 19 Royal Navy
 16 RAF [until 1 April 1918 Royal Flying Corps]
 12 Canadian
 11 Australian
  4 Royal Marines
  2 Queen Mary's Army Auxiliary Corps
  1 South Africans
  1 Women's Royal Air Force
  5 Interned German civilians
 45 German Army

A Permanent Memorial

It was decided at a public meeting that a permanent memorial to the town's dead was needed. It was agreed that Lord Lilford would be the president of the memorial fund and he personally pledged £50 towards the fund. The memorial would mark not only the men of Northampton who fell during the Great War but men from throughout the county. Initially funds were raised for a monument in or around Abington Park and a memorial hall that would fit 2,000 people. However, many people thought that this was an unfair proposal made by the wealthy 'east-enders' and that the memorial would be better placed in front of the Guildhall. Various proposals were put forward by members of the public and suggestions ranged in scale and scope. One design was for a neoclassical arch to span the top of the Guildhall Road.

The Town and County Memorial.

The required funds were soon raised and it was eventually decided that a memorial was to be erected in the grounds of All Saints church, facing Wood Hill. Designed by the renowned architect Sir Edwin Lutyens, who was responsible for the design of the Cenotaph in London and was also one of the founding members of the Imperial War Graves Commission, the Northampton monument was unveiled in 1926 by General Lord Horne and was to be known as the Town and County Memorial. Central to the war memorial is the stone of sacrifice, which bears the inscription 'Their Name Liveth for Evermore'. These words, found on many war memorials, came from the poet and author Rudyard Kipling, who himself had lost his son Jack during the war.

Thankful Villages

The Town and County Memorial pays homage to the men of Northamptonshire who went to fight for King and Country but never returned. Men from every town, village and hamlet are represented by the memorial, except for two 'thankful villages'. East Carlton, near Corby, and Woodend, near Towcester, lost no men during the war and their villages – unlike most others in the country – have no war memorial to the fallen. They do, however, have plaques that remember those that went to war and to give thanks for their safe return.

A thankful village. This plaque at St Peter's church, East Carlton, gives thanks that all of those that went to fight returned safely home.

Garden of Remembrance

In 1937 the Garden of Remembrance was opened in Abington Square, Northampton. It marked the completion of a long campaign, headed by the British Legion, to get a permanent memorial listing the names of the 2,906 men who never returned to their hometown. Unlike the Town and County Memorial, the wall of remembrance was specifically for the men of the town. The large sum required to compete the memorial was raised by public subscriptions. The memorial is inscribed: 'County Borough of Northampton. Here are inscribed the names of the citizens of this borough who gave their lives during the Great War, 1914–1918. This memorial was erected during the Coronation Year of His Majesty King George VI. Lest we forget.'

The Garden of Remembrance was opened by Major General Sir John Brown, deputy director of the Territorial Forces, and head of the firm Messrs John Brown and Henson architects, St Giles Street. He was also the chief architect responsible for the design. Some 1,200 ex-servicemen, led by the band of the British Legion, paraded through the town and made their way to the new memorial. The ceremony opened with the hymn 'O Valiant Hearts' and was followed by an address by Major General Brown. As well as looking back on the past, Brown's address highlighted the developing situation in Europe and asked the question, 'Now the point is, are we who are left worthy of their sacrifice …?'

The Mobbs Memorial

Upon hearing of the death of Edgar Mobbs, a town meeting was held to discuss a memorial 'to perpetuate the memory of the late Lieutenant Colonel Mobbs'. A memorial fund was agreed and £250 was pledged by the end of the meeting. Within a fortnight a sum of over £1,100 had been raised. The large amount raised in such a short space of time shows how well regarded Mobbs was by the inhabitants of Northampton.

The job of creating the memorial went to the sculpture Alfred Turner, who fashioned a bronze bust of Mobbs, which was crowned with a depiction of the goddess of fame. Other reliefs carry the theme of sport and war and the inscription reads:

> In memory of Edgar R. Mobbs DSO, erected by subscriptions of admirers the world over, to the memory of a great and gallant soldier sportsman. When the Great War broke out he founded 'Mobbs Company', joined as a private and rose to command a battalion to which it belonged. He did his duty even unto death.

In July 1921, eighty-five veterans of D Company, 7th Battalion Northamptonshire Regiment, marched through the town as part of the unveiling ceremony preceded over by Lord Lilford. The

EDGAR MOBBS' MEMORIAL, NORTHAMPTON.

memorial was originally located in the Wood Hill entrance to the Market Square but was moved to the Garden of Remembrance in the 1930s to allow motorised traffic greater access to the square. In addition to the physical memorial, Mobbs is remembered in other ways: a Mobbs memorial match is still played every year and there is a street near to the home of Northampton Saints at Franklin's Garden named after him.

Walter Tull

Not all memorials to the casualties of the Great War were erected in the years immediately following the end of the conflict. In contrast to the rest of the town's memorials, which were erected at a time when the First World War was still in most people's living memories, Walter Tull's memorial was unveiled on 11 July 1999 at Sixfields Stadium. The memorial was erected in recognition of his bravery on the battlefield, his leadership abilities and his spirit in overcoming prejudice, both as a black footballer and as the army's first British-born black officer. The memorial reads:

> Through his actions, W.D.J. Tull ridiculed the barriers of ignorance that tried to deny people of colour equality with their contemporaries. His life stands testament to a determination to confront those people and those obstacles that sought to diminish him and the world in which he lived. It reveals a man, though rendered breathless in his prime, whose strong heart still beats loudly.

The Walter Tull memorial at the entrance to the Cobblers ground at Sixfields.

Legacy of the Regiments

After the Great War, the Northamptonshire Regiment went on to fight gallantly in the Middle East, Italy and north-west Europe during the Second World War. In 1960 the regiment was amalgamated with the Royal Lincolnshire Regiment and became the 2nd East Anglian Regiment (Duchess of Gloucester's Own Royal Lincolnshire and Northamptonshire). It was then changed again in 1964 and became the 2nd Battalion (Duchess of Gloucester's Own Royal Lincolnshire and Northamptonshire), Royal Anglian Regiment. Following further changes in 1992 and 1995 the regiment has become (Northamptonshire) Company Royal Anglian Regiment.

In 1922 the Northamptonshire Yeomanry reluctantly traded their horses in for armoured vehicles. During the Second World War the regiment used Cromwell and Sherman tanks during the campaign in north-west Europe from 1944 to 1945. In 1961, as a result of defence cuts and reorganisation, the regiment became 250 (Northamptonshire Yeomanry) Independent Field Squadron, Royal Engineers. By 1967 the regiment had become A Company (Northamptonshire Yeomanry), Northamptonshire Regiment.

Anyone wishing to discover more about the history of either the Northamptonshire Regiment or the Northamptonshire Yeomanry can visit the regimental collections at the Abington Park Museum, where the memories of those who gave the ultimate sacrifice in the Great War are kept alive.

Lest we forget.

IN LOVING REMEMBRANCE OF

Pte. WALTER TARRY,
1/4th Northants. Regt.,

The beloved and youngest son of
John and Mary Ann Tarry,

Who died of wounds
received in action at Gaza,
on April 19th, 1917.

In his 22nd year.

When alone in my sorrow, and bitter
    tears flow,
There stealeth sweet dreams of a short
    time ago;
And, unknown to the world, he stands
    by my side,
And whispers these words "Death
    cannot divide."

Fondly we loved him—he is dear to us
    still—
But in grief we must bend to God's
    holy will,
Our sorrow is great, our loss hard to
    bear,
But the angels, dear brother, will guard
    guard you with care.

69, Edith Street,
Northampton.

BIBLIOGRAPHY

Primary Sources

Bassett-Lowke Catalogue, No. 196

Bassett-Lowke Ltd, *50 Years of Model Making: The Story of Bassett-Lowke from the Turn of the Century*

Bemrose, Sandra, *Diary of Sister 'Dolly' Derham*

Northamptonshire Regimental Collection (held by Northampton Museums and Art Gallery)

Veterans' interviews – Sound Archive: Imperial War Museums

Secondary Sources

Bemrose, Sandra, *St Crispin Hospital, 1876–1995* (2008)

Bucknell, John, *Service, Sacrifice and Survival: Weston Favel in the First World War* (2012)

Cazenove, H. de L., *Northamptonshire Yeomanry 1794–1964* (Private Printing, 1966)

Chapman, Colin R., and S. Richard Moss, *Detained in England, 1914–1920: Eastcote POW Camp Pattishall* (Lochin Publishing, 2012)

Crutchley, Charles, *Shilling a Day Soldier* (New Horizon, 1980)

DeGroot, Gerard J., *Blighty: British Society in the Era of the Great War* (Longman, 1996)

Dewey, Peter, *War and Progress: Britain 1914–1945* (Routledge, 1996)

Fegan, Thomas, *The 'Baby Killers': German Air Raids on Britain in the First World War* (Pen & Sword Military, 2013)

Gullace, Nicoletta F., *White Feathers and Wounded Men: Female Patriotism and the Memory of the Great War* (Cambridge University Press, 1997)

Hammerson, Michael, *No Easy Hopes or Lies: The World War One Letters of Lt Arthur Preston White* (London Stamp Exchange, 1991)

Hatley, V.A. and J. Rajczonek, 'Shoemakers in Northamptonshire 1762–1911: A Statistical Survey', *Northampton Historical Series*, No. 6 (1971)